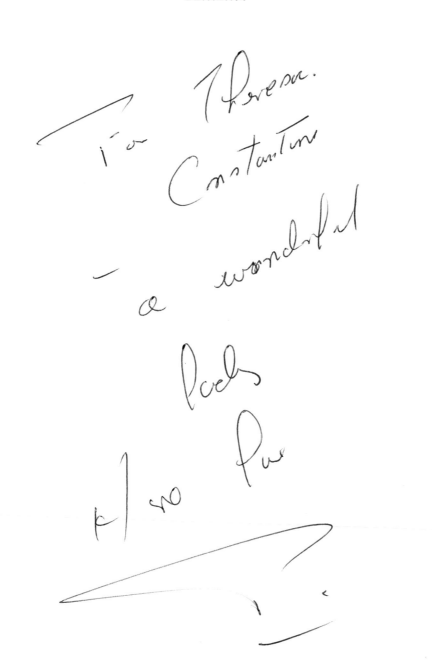

To Theresa.
Constantine
— a wonderful
a
Poets
Also Por

K...I...S...S

a meditation on the art of well being by
"keeping it simple"

by

Peter Stanley

who would like you to kiss goodbye
to all your troubles anyway.

With Foreword by Dr. Helen Carey PhD

YOUCAXTON
PUBLICATIONS

This is for all my family

for

Roger and Gaye

George, Abby, Ada

and of course for Tom

for Penny and all her family

for all my cousins, second cousins

for all those that I considered my family

that is those I worked with, my employees and colleagues

and for Oliver just arrived

but most of all

for

Mame

Acknowledgements

So many of you, thank you, each and everyone, especially those whom I have not mentioned but you know how much I appreciate your help. First though must be Doctor Alan Gainer and his wife Edna, thank you for your insight, your trust and your kindness. Then those lovely editors, Gaye and Madge who together with Helen Carey liberally kicked my backside and seemed to put red lines through every page, George who started the red ink splurge and then, starting with Rowan Hisayo Buchanan, all those authors in residence at Gladstone's library in Hawarden. The Warden Rector of Gladstone's, now retired, Peter Francis. Roger for his patience, Carol Harris, Megan Close Zavala of Turn The Page Book Coaching and Editorial, Harry Bingham and all his staff at Jericho Writers, also Ricardo and all the staff at Reedsy, Amy Shone, Emma and Simon Wells, Bob Fowke, Ella Knight and all the staff at You Caxton, John Smith, June Eades, Gerald and Elizabeth Dobson, Lisa Roxburgh, my sister Penny and all my ever patient family, and of course, to Mame.

Acknowledgements

Foreword

We are in an age where evidence based knowledge founded through robust research methods are encouraged, celebrated and acted upon. No more so than in how humans can achieve longevity of life with maximum health. We are consistently advised what we should do, and what others should do to us, in order to receive the golden prize of healthy longevity in life. Yet the best method of learning is to view through an example. May I introduce you to Peter and "Keep it Simple"

It is entirely appropriate that health is now discussed in the wider term of well-being. Well-being can be achieved when people are able to carry out the activities they need or wish to do without undue consideration of their physical, mental and social capacities, and when the environment they are in allows such activity. In other words, well-being is to be able to participate in life how we want to be able to. So, evidence based practice now focuses on measuring us in terms of well-being.

There is an abundance of well-being measures and also quality of life measures. We are now advised what we should and should not do to achieve well-being. Yet, the best method of learning is to view through an example. May I again, introduce you to Peter and "Keep it Simple"

I first met Peter at our gym swimming pool. A gentlemen of mature years who swims, walks, talks, listens and laughs with great enthusiasm. If there is an image and a high measure of well-being, then it is Peter. So who best to learn how to achieve the golden prize of healthy longevity in life? Who better to teach how we can emulate well-being?

I write this foreword two months after moving to America to commence an Associate Professorship Occupational Therapy post in Florida. I promised Peter this would be written within a fortnight of my arrival but it has been delayed a little - Corona Virus has infiltrated the globe. The health of global mankind is threatened; at best the outcome will be a shaking of global economics and an understanding that we cannot take our fragility on this earth for granted, at worst this could change our societies for the future. At the time of reading this book, you will know which occurred. However, throughout this present chaos, I find myself often thinking what would Peter say now? What would Peter do? Positive examples guide us.

As you read this book I encourage you to keep some theory in mind. Firstly, we are what we do. Mary Reilly in 1962 stated that "Man, through the use of his hands as they are energized by his mind and will, can influence the state of his own health". Peter describes what he has done through his life, and how his doing has energized both him and others around him. Motivation, or what Mary describes as "will", is a key element throughout Peter's story.

Self determination theory, devised by Deci and Ryan in 2012, considers that people are motivated through a combination of intrinsic and extrinsic factors coinciding, but the primary motivator is enjoyment. Peter shows a thirst for enjoyment, a thirst that continues throughout his life journey, and most importantly, a recognition of fulfillment. Many of us continue to strive for the ultimate in enjoyment but never feel we find it. Peter gains fulfillment in the journey.

Secondly, we should do what we like doing. Consider the concept of occupational flow. Csikszenmihaly, in 1990, studied people involved in doing and found that when they were involved in challenging and absorbing activities which were well suited to them personally, they experienced a joyful state which he termed "flow". In a state of flow we are significantly more happy, strong, satisfied, creative and concentrated. We are completely immersed in what we are doing, therefore we become free in our thinking and our activities become less effort to us. Peter shows us how to achieve occupational flow.

Finally, the impact of what we do cascades to others. De Groot in 2015 demonstrated that feelings of happiness transfer between individuals through mimicry, and many others have studied how a person in a group task can increase feelings of positivity, and enhance the efficiency of a task. Such instances show a cascade impact - one person's positive act transmits to another who does a positive act and so on, otherwise termed positive emotional contagion! There are many examples of when health care professionals speak in terms of "can do" to their patients, their well-being is increased. Peter shows us how applying the positive to a situation cascades to more positivity in others.

So, three theories to think about; we are what we do, we should do what we like doing and when we do this, we impact positively on others. Now I will pass you over to the master of putting these three theories in practice, I pass you to Peter........

Dr Helen Carey

Associate Professor University of St Augustine for Health Sciences, Florida USA.

Professional Lead in Occupational Therapy at Glyndwr University, Wales, UK.

PhD, MSc Adv OT, Dip COT, OTR, OTL

26th March 2020

Csikszenmihaly M (1990) Flow: The Psychology of Optimal Experiences. Psychological Studies of Flow in Consciousness. New York. Harper and Row.

Deci, E.L., and Ryan, R.M., (2012) Motivation, personality and development with embedded social constructs: An overview of self determination theory. In Ryan, R.M. (ed.) Oxford Handbook of Human Motivation. Oxford. OxfordUniversity Press. Pp85-101.

De Groot, J.H.B., Smeets, N.A.M., Rowson, M.J., Bulsing, P.J., Blonk, C.G., Wilkinsn, J., Semon, G.R. (2015) A sniff of happiness. Psychology. Vol 25, No 6, pp 85-101

Reilly, M. (1962) Occupational therapy can be one of the greatest ideas of the 20th century medicine. American Journal of Occupational Therapy.

Contents

CHAPTER 1

What's it all about then?

The more that we care for the happiness of others, the greater is the sense of our own well being – HH The Dalai Lama

Do you want to live forever? Probably not with all the problems that seem to pursue us all these days; maybe you have just got in from a hectic day, been stuck in traffic, you want a cup of tea, the kettle's just blown a fuse – so you do as well. Familiar? Don't worry, it happens to all of us. You might be the Prime Minister and told that half your supporters want you out, which is exactly what the leader of the opposition has also been told. Or the kids have played up – or the kids you teach at school have played up – or you've left your homework on the bus – or the care home that you have just moved to is going to shut down – perhaps you've just been born and wonder what on earth it's all about.

Wait a minute, what's the title of this book? K.I.S.S , it stands for 'keep it simple stupid' and I've just broken that first rule, I haven't kept it simple! OK, so it's all about rule breaking then; actually that is how I get into so much trouble. I do break rules, constantly, and I must admit that this does, sometimes, cause a little bit of suffering, not just to myself but to others. This is amply illustrated the further you read.

So is this a book then about the relief of suffering? Yes, I hope so, but it should be read just for pleasure, for amusement and maybe some little mistake that I have made or some quixotic or stupid action taken without consideration for the consequences will ring a warning bell and maybe, perhaps, which is my hope, it may well be of some help to you in some small, undefined way.

This then is primarily a memoir, a way of life that not many others would choose to follow but if it is to mean anything, then it is worth while getting this down in writing so that some of the incidents related, which may now seem hilarious but at the time were probably quite the opposite, can possibly enable you, as the reader, to benefit by avoiding the little traps that we all fall into from time to time.

The trouble is that many of us are a little careless with our own well being, and in particular, our health. It is now approaching something like fifty years since Alan, a doctor at the practice where I was registered in Shropshire, who became an exceptionally good friend, not on the squash court I may add, told me that if I could get down in book form what I did to get rid of illness in myself then I would get 80% of the patients out of his surgery. I then asked my mother what she did to cure herself as I wanted to enable this gift, as did Alan, to be available to everyone, maybe in some book form, perhaps on tape, any way at all so that it would be of benefit for others; she replied "you just do it". When I gently suggested that this possibly needed a little further expansion she said "everyone does it, you don't need doctors".

I did try to point out that I did not think that to be the case but it was to no avail. She had a very strong mind and it paid not to try to dissuade her, so I set about putting it down on paper by myself. Absolutely impossible, very easy for my mother, Elizabeth Helene, nicknamed Bits and myself to undertake, but dealing with illness in this way is something that you practice, that you experience and not something that you can easily pick up from the spoken or written word.

So far I have not been able to devise a method of communicating in written form this way of eliminating or mitigating illness. The best way to deal with illness is to prevent it but it becomes a tad more difficult if your genes dictate otherwise. However I do hope that some of the ways that I have used to prevent, help or mitigate the effects of disease, illness, ill health, aging or simply the sheer grind of daily living can be of some help in the following pages.

OK, why the title? KISS is the acronym that you teach all sales people BUT it should be taught to EVERYONE – why? because *keep it simple stupid* is a constant reminder to all of us not to clutter our minds with thoughts or plans that distract from our main objective. Mindfulness in all it's various forms. Do I practice it? I try, but I talk too much on occasions, I am also afraid that I do tend to get distracted and get off the subject. Well, after all, I am male and can only ever do one thing at a time, so if you distract me then I am bound to forget what I'm doing. It also happens as you get older. It also occurs if you are a bit stupid as well.

I have no magic wand, no secret formula but what I can do is simply enumerate a way of life that I undertook, a few funny incidents with the great and the good (and the not so good). I have already chosen the inscription for my headstone - 'at least he tried'. That will do for this as well.

This is a book then about a rebel who lived a crazy life, about illness, business, self help, laughter but hopefully, something much more important; as an antidote to the suffering which we all experience – Buddhist advocate the Noble Eightfold Path, Chinese The Tao, Japanese Zen, the list goes on and on – has anyone yet come up with an answer? Not really, but if you read on then at least YOU may be able to if something in the following pages just tweaks that inner spark which you have within you, and enlightens you sufficiently to be able to elucidate for all of us.

Helen always elucidates the art of well being to her students and very kindly, having arrived in Florida with her husband Andrew only to find themselves right at the start of the corona virus pandemic, wrote in her foreword "what would Peter do now, what would Peter say?" I can tell her because it is how I try to live my life anyway, simply in this very moment; yesterdays gone, tomorrow hasn't come yet so all that you have is just this one actual moment, nothing else. I usually end all my emails, letters and communications with "have fun" – or "much love" – or "with my very kindest regards" and try to live up to this by treating every day as if it were my last day on earth, have as much fun as possible, with as much love as possible, for all those around me, and with my very kindest regards, here the emphasis is on the word kindest or, effectively, kindness, for everyone else. Does it work? Well it does for me so I have simply set out in the following pages what I do in order to achieve this state.

Will it work for you? May I again say, please, do not contemplate copying what I did because I got into so much trouble along the way, so just take from it what you need. There is that lovely saying that if you wish to find your way to the top of the mountain then ask someone who has been there. They can show you the way, they can give directions and indicate the best paths to follow, but they cannot make the journey for you. You have to do that yourself. Very true.

Helen also mentioned 'flow'. Occupational flow occurs when you are thoroughly engaged in the task that you are undertaking, upon which you are focused and which has purpose and meaning for YOU. There could be many reasons why you are focused but the focus comes from whatever it is that motivates you; my belief is that the secret of "flow" is in finding exactly that. Helen finds flow from her role of leadership in her work and she also finds flow from being with her family, but in the pandemic that was not possible, so I simply suggested that she tried to find some fun. We can find 'flow' in having fun, enjoyment is such an important element of flow. Making you way to the top of the mountain is that much easier when you do so with "flow", you enjoy the journey as well as the destination. There are also pitfalls on that journey, but we have all experienced those precipices and crevasses – and, at the risk of repeating myself yet again, I am certainly no exception as you will discover the further that you read !!

Helen throws everything she can at the task in hand when leading her team. Headhunted from the Countess of Chester Hospital, she always had the distinction of being the number one in the country for the disciplines that she led at Glyndwr university. Her husband is a talented football coach who, when they landed in Florida at the start of the pandemic, took the team that engaged him from nothing to winning their league, all in one season. None of this achieved without just a little trauma and personal sacrifice.

For me, flow still comes despite what you may imagine as an impossible period in your life. My belief is also that it will come if you perform a task to the uttermost of your ability, with all your heart and with total integrity. If you are in a position of leadership then have no thought for yourself but for those whom you lead. This applies in exactly the same way if you are the CEO (Chief Executive Officer) of a top 100 company or are a housewife with a family who depend on you.

Anything else? - yes, the journey to the top of the mountain is always much easier if you practice kindness, put yourself last, have total acceptance of whatever is thrown at you and have no attachment, I'll explain this later, to any idea, to any possession or indeed to life itself, but do endeavour to love, love with all your heart and -oh- never forget, have fun along the way!!

CHAPTER 2

Why do some of us beat ourselves up and some of us beat others

There are only two ways to live your life. One is as though nothing is a miracle, the other is though everything is a miracle. -
Albert Einstein 1879-1955

What do we all have in common? Is it that in every single family there is always at least one person who beats themselves up? The funny thing is that we all know that it is stupid, we all know exactly what to do to stop it and what to do if it happens anyway. That is, we know the theory but that is one heck of a long way from actually doing it; it was always drummed into me that knowledge is one thing, but it is the application and the ability to apply that knowledge that really matters.

I was extremely fortunate in having had superb support for myself. My wife, Mame, served with the Samaritans for nine years, and in my personal opinion they were exceptionally successful in helping people in distress, never being judgmental, and always offering a listening ear or a helping hand. Mame ended up as a local director in the south west and their friends fund raising events were wonderful to attend as their dedication, commitment, and sheer well being for everyone shone through with total naturalness. I also saw this wish to care, or assist others, in my daughter, Gaye, who looks after people with learning difficulties, but who also holds meditation classes in Heartfullness, and is a Yoga teacher. She has two somewhat rather special boys, George and Tom, who she brought up on her own following the death of their father, Alan. They have all done exceptionally well in their own individual and accomplished ways.

Let me stick in a little word of explanation here: I am an optimist, I view everything through those rose coloured glasses, and the one thing that I do not want in this book is a single trace of negativity. So when I am referring to my family then I probably double up on those rose tinted glasses, *(or quadruple them – editor)*. If it makes anyone sound too good to be true then let me say that I can totally infuriate just about every single member of my family exactly as they all do to me at various times. We are all human, at least until AI (artificial intelligence) finally takes over - Just joking – I hope !

My son, Roger, highly intelligent but exceptionally kind, was busy turning a small farm into a wildlife sanctuary and had just planted 3,000 trees. He rang up one day and said "Dad, we've just bought a farm". At the time he was leading a very different life in Moscow. Mame always said that he must have been a 'spook' as we never, ever, really found out what he actually did, for that matter neither did his wife, Ruth. However Ruth had a superb calming effect on all whom she met so perhaps she actually teased an answer out of him, but somehow I doubt it.

Let's complete the family, my sister Penny is always helping others by volunteering for some good cause or another. She was managing the local Citizens Advice Bureau and, having retired, went straight back as a volunteer. She was married to Don who died quite recently, but he always assisted those in difficulty, especially with organisations such as the Scouts, and on many occasions lent a helping hand with an ever open ear for those young people requiring guidance. They also have a couple of great children and grandchildren.

I am also very fortunate as all my cousins/second cousins are workaholics like myself but very caring and most community minded. However when we do all meet up and there are now 60 to 80 of us, we do find striking similarities with basic personality traits. However it would take up far too many pages to list everyone, also you would become very bored!.

So that's what it's about then, let's play happy families and get rid of all the unhappiness and misery. Replace the doom and gloom with a positive attitude. Not quite that easy. Let's start with beating ourselves up, we've all done it, but this book is not about some crackpot idea that will overturn millions of years of breeding, genetics, DNA which together with Darwin's natural selection discoveries dictate whether we are tall or short, male or female, happy or unhappy: no matter how clever we think we are to have adjusted to our environment, and our way of coping with life, our genes may well tell us something totally different.

Why the long title for this chapter, perhaps I am just trying to get your attention as I would particularly like to highlight the work that was carried out by Mame in such an exemplary fashion. I also happen to have just read the following article in the Daily Telegraph on Thursday the Thirteenth. Tomorrow is Good Friday and I guess that that is quite symbolic. Victoria Lambert writes of the Wilson family whose 17 year old son, Nathan, committed suicide and whom they feel was badly let down by various authorities who were most probably short of cash, short of staff, and ticking boxes on forms instead of making face to face contact. "We tried over and over to get help but we've been ignored" said the Wilson's.

It is a very tragic tale, Nathan's mother, Gail, stated "Nathan once said to me that he wanted his life to mean something. We have to speak up about the system as this may be of help to other parents. If it is then his life will have been short, but it will have been full of value". Victoria goes on to say that the Wilson's experience is far from unusual as suicide is the largest single killer of males under 45 in the UK. Could all this have been prevented? Well that is something over which we can only speculate, but what I most earnestly hope is that with the Wilson family supporting the charity Papyrus in their current endeavours, then this will assist other families who may find themselves in a similar situation. It will certainly go a long way in ensuring that Nathan's life has indeed been of exceptional value.

So what of those who beat themselves up then, what of those who beat others up and what about the lucky ones who do neither and simply fill the middle ground. Well I'm sure we've all been guilty of beating ourselves up at some time or another. Exceptions being full blown psychopaths (because they have no conscience) and saints. However a rather special lady, Mother Theresa of Calcutta, did beat herself up at one stage over doubts about her own faith, and belief in God; but she was still ordained as a Saint anyway.

What about those who beat up others, the bullies. Perhaps they are actually afraid themselves? the fear syndrome, ego, and a degree of being on the psychopath scale must surely also be present to some degree. How about those who come somewhere in between? The lucky ones are those who are so emotionally stable that highs and lows are rarely experienced. They tread a middle path, equally balanced at all times. That's OK as long as they realise that they are in the middle of the road, and that they continually keep on the look out for some thundering great truck who simply comes along, doesn't see them and then that's goodnight. Mixed metaphors and mayhem. In other words, we never know what is around the corner, it could be a sudden illness, or just the problem of getting older.

We all live longer now but is that quality of life continuing in the same way to keep pace with the advancement in medical methods? The problem of debilitating age related conditions for which there is no cure. As is the case today for so many illnesses for which there is no remedy accept to ease the pain; this applies to all generations and is probably most distressing for those with young children. As was related in that Telegraph article regarding the Wilson family that I mentioned previously.

CHAPTER 3

Physician heal thyself

Luke 4:23

So how did I deal with illness? Let's start at the beginning. I was born on the 28th June 1933 in Ealing, West London , diagnosed with a whole variety of minor ailments, and one of my first memories is that of being in Great Ormond Street Hospital before the war where I learnt total respect for the position of matron. In those days Matron's word was law, and although they appeared stern beyond belief, it was for everyone's benefit; respect and obedience were absolute. I was also to learn of the superb service given by all those in the health care system, a view that has not altered in any way at all over the last, what is now approaching, ninety years.

Maybe there was also another reason for everyone diagnosing me as timid and frail. I am two or three years old, the nightmares are horrific, I am continually attacked by blinding lights. And they hurt. They hurt a lot and I am really scared, there is no where to hide, I simply cower. In my dreams the light bulbs come down from their sockets and attack me. One of my very first memories is that of waking in the early hours of the morning and of slowly, like a fledgling sparrow tumbling out of its' nest, coming down the stairs at our house in Acton, and my father trying to help. I remember him taking a bulb from it's socket, and attempting to show me that it was harmless, one of my very first memories indeed. The nightmares continued though. That was until I had a little inner voice saying "they are the lights, they are all seeing, you can defeat them, you are their Prince, you can be their King". Where all this came from I have no idea, at the age of three or coming up to four, time moves at a slower pace and knowledge is scarce, and it is scattered.

Gradually I came, in my dreams, to face them; then I was given a shining sword from where I know not, this I gripped tightly and without further thought I sprang, I attacked and then they cowered, and then they vanished, not immediately but over a number of dreams. I have no explanation for any of this, I have never told anyone so there may well be a simple answer, maybe that is part of what makes up the reason for dreaming, possibly a form of training, education, maybe forewarned is forearmed. I have no idea, answers on a postcard please.

Having been told that I was too frail for this, too frail for that, and confined to bed for long periods of time, I devised various ways of dealing with each situation. One of which was to stare very firmly, these days I would probably say 'meditate on' rather than 'stare at', the bed knobs at the foot of my metal framed bed, when the treatment for one of my so called ailments or disabilities, such as Asthma, was to be confined to bed for a minimum of two weeks at a time. I would repeat to myself, over and over again, "I have not got Asthma". "I will not have this….." I later learnt about the power of affirmation – people such as Emile Coue – but I was certainly not aware of him in those days and at that age. I always think of him now as the father of positive thinking, a very famous French psychologist who coined the phrase *"tous les tours a tous points de vue je vais de mieux en mieux"*- "every day in every way I'm getting better and better".

It was firmly explained to me, years later, that I simply grew out of having asthma and that may well be the case. However it is only a couple of years ago when Mame and I were having a meal with our friends, Alan and Edna, the doctor and his wife, when I said to Alan "When my mother cured herself of her Cancer that was diagnosed as incurable, it was probably just a misdiagnosis in the first place". He replied "not at all, you may remember that I was also an anesthetist as well as a GP, and we have many instances where the X Rays and Scans show that the condition is terminal, so we have no option but to diagnose that the patient may only have just a few weeks to live. We have no explanation for when, in six months time, the X Rays and scans show a greatly reduced tumor or indeed no tumor at all". He went on to say that they simply treat each instance as beyond their field of knowledge or experience, but acknowledge that this is not restricted to isolated instances.

I have had many occasions where no rational explanation is possible, but I too never bother to delve any further, I just accept, and am grateful for the experience. Dr D.B.Nugegoda in his book *Overcoming Psychological Stress* cites Siegel (1993): "So ....as a young man he wanted to become a violinist when he grew up. Due to parental pressure he became a lawyer, which profession he disliked. After some time he developed a brain cancer and doctors had given him one year to live. Not getting depressed, which usually would have been the case, he used the opportunity to play the violin and became a violinist. With this his tumor disappeared"................

I seem to have spent considerable time in medical establishments one way and the other, especially latterly when I was a full time carer for my wife Mame for four years, and part time caring for considerably longer. In my younger days, the facilities available were not as they are today, but I have always found over the whole length of my life that the commitment of all medical staff to the six C's of Nursing has been absolute; what are the six C's? - Care, Courage, Compassion, Commitment, Communication, Competence, but I also add a seventh – Consideration. Many deride the NHS, but having now been privileged to have sat on a number of Patient Panels I find the 'knockers' somewhat tiresome, and just a little self serving.

When I first told my son Roger that I was going to sit on an NHS patient panel he told me that I was crazy if I thought that I could do anything to change a monolithic giant like the NHS. I believe that we did achieve much, particularly by encouraging responsible positive thinking. I say responsible because although I am the most ardent supporter of positive thinking, in no way do I think that it can replace sound medical knowledge, nor the superb advancements that medical science has achieved over recent decades. What it can do is greatly assist the healing process when used in conjunction with medical dictates.

Steve Jobs achieved miracles with Apple, however I think that he went a little too far when he elected to cure his cancer with just the power of his mind alone; also some of his way out notions regarding the curative powers of his self inflicted diet. He ended up six foot under. There is the excellent story of the Tibetan Yogi who was studying under Milarepa, and who went off for twenty years of solitary meditation in a cave in order to see if he would be able to walk on water. After 20 years he went back to the great man and said "Master, I have now learned to walk on water". The rejoinder was "Well you're a fool because you have wasted 20 years. You could have given the ferryman a few coins and he would have carried you across".

The lesson is simple, that is probably the correct word as well. KISS should always be applied – *Keep It Simple* – If medical science has an effective answer then use it, do things the easy way. Regretfully I am writing those words knowing full well that I nearly always do exactly the opposite. I'll blame genetics, I probably take after my mother!

Is there any scientific proof as regards the power of positive thinking? Absolutely, do have a look online at the natural therapy pages of Australia's No 1 Natural Therapy Site. There was also a little contribution from the Telegraph again which cited research from Stanford University, where a study of 60,000 people showed some fascinating results by people who simply 'thought themselves fit'. The Australian web site quoted such eminent experts as Dr Dacher Keltner of the University of California who maintained that Darwin, far from expounding 'survival of the fittest' actually postulated that 'sympathy is our greatest instinct'. The main points from the field of positive psychology were:

- ***Happiness is the CAUSE of positive outcomes in life NOT the result***

13

- *Happy people tend to have deep religious or spiritual beliefs*
- *Wealth does not bring happiness but using one's wealth to benefit others does contribute to personal happiness*
- *Altruism is a surer road to happiness than hedonism*
- *Happiness (or positive thinking) is a "skill" that can be learned.*

Having learned, inherited or simply intuitively deduced a method of getting rid of, or reducing the impact of certain health issues, I set about building a structure that would limit or negate their impact should they or some other nasty bug like condition rear its ugly head. Again this is very basic: Exercise: Eat the right foods: Exercise: Keep your weight under control: Exercise: Watch those stress levels .... however my belief is that the most important ingredient of all is to have the right attitude of mind.

CHAPTER 4

Attitude and Belief

As you sow, so shall you reap - Galatians 6:7

How do you develop the right attitude of mind? Having touched on positive thinking let's have a look at a few other methods that many people say that they find helpful, Belief systems, the Power of Prayer, Meditation, Nutrition, Exercise, but lets start with Yoga. There is a very special practitioner based in Bristol called Saeed Ansari. He comes from a long line of Yogis in India, in the whole of his life he has never been angry.

He once came to a business meeting with me. I was one of the speakers, the chair was Sir Roger Cork of Cork Gully, and latterly Lord Mayor of London. Sir Roger turned to me at the coffee break and said "Peter, for goodness sake do something to liven things up, and can you speak for two hours please". I had prepared for an hour – and that's long enough for one person. No Power Point in those days!

This was at Exeter University, and we had the South West's leading insolvency lawyers, insolvency practitioners, accountants and credit managers in the audience. I was speaking on management and motivation. When one of the audience asked a question regarding stress in the work place, I said "the best person to answer that is Saeed who is a practising Yogi, so I wonder, Saeed, if you could come up and give us the benefit of how you see this?".

Saeed came up, smiled at the audience who were all most smartly dressed (you can tell that it was a long time ago) and said "you have all been sitting on your bottoms far too long, stand up and we will start with the breath". Stunned silence, up stands Sir Roger, off with his jacket displaying the city's formal attire of deep red bracer's, and he then instructed the audience "come on! - all of you follow Saeed". Off came the jackets and ties, and Saeed had everyone in the room participating in exercises to get the circulation going, and breathing exercises for relaxation. It turned into the most enlightening business conference in a long while. The press cuttings stated that "Saeed's ten minutes were not nearly enough, his talk was electrifying"; yes it was, but not only did he fill in for the time lapse, he pinched a whole load of my time as well!! Never be upstaged by animals, children or Yogis! There are many definitions of Yoga, many people think of it as a way to suppleness, I tell people that it is what I try to undertake every waking minute whilst at work or play, Saeed puts this more eloquently:

Yoga is your natural state. You cannot do yoga. What you can do are physical yoga exercises which may reveal to you where you are resisting your natural state while performing a yoga posture. Our natural state is not about resisting, but letting go of the resistance. Compassion, kindness and love are our natural state. Consequently yoga is not about straining, it is about sustaining; yoga is not about achieving, it is about accepting; yoga is not about looking good, it is about feeling good. This is my simple definition of yoga. The literal translation from *Sanskrit* is 'union' and Saeed is an amazing example of the correct way to join together the different facets of daily living in order to develop the right attitude of mind.

OK, how about belief systems? my own belief system is simple, wherever I am in the world, be it Christian, Jewish, Islamic or, when I used to go to Russia many years ago when it was a communist country (the belief system was Karl Marx as adapted by the ruling hierarchy) then I would also totally respect their system. In whichever country I ended up I would attend the applicable place of worship, a mosque or a synagogue perhaps, simply as a visitor, not participant, but never did I attempt to put forward my own views, and NEVER belittle or denigrate the belief of the person to whom I was talking.

This has always been a cardinal rule of mine ever since I can remember. You can destroy a person very easily by some ill considered remark. We all have a belief system or none at all as some people say. Whatever it is, I will always respect it. When once addressing a group in Russia, when they had nothing, I was asked what my faith was and why I came to Russia to do what I did; in other words why go to a country that you did not know, a people with different customs, different beliefs, and where there was really no prospect of material reward, but simply to help someone less fortunate than yourself.

Difficult question – why did I ? - but for that matter why do highly paid doctors give their services for free to Medicines sans Frontieres, why do we have so many young people going abroad to help in countries such as Sierra Leone with the overseas volunteer service, which my grandson Tom did when he went to Africa? I believe that it is a spiritual matter, better to give than to receive. If you do someone a bad turn it comes back tenfold but if you do someone a good turn it comes back a hundredfold. Again my belief is that this is a good principle, but if you are in doubt and want proof, then simply just give it a try. I also believe that if you have certain talents then you should share them, in the long run the returns are huge though not necessarily in material terms. Ask Bill or Melinda Gates why they do what they do. Ask any volunteer with our most numerous charities, Lifeboats, for those in distress upon the seas, Samaritans for those who are suicidal or mentally troubled, Shelter for those who are homeless.

I replied to the Russians who had been living under a feudal system for around 900 years before they hit on the idea of all being equal (which didn't really work out as they swapped a Tsar for a dictator) that my belief system was to simply respect each other persons belief, nothing more, and as I was in their country, then I had total respect for communism, but that I did not personally practice it.

Then another question, was I a good person. I'd had a few sessions like this when you begin to wonder if the people you are addressing are all KGB, not simply the ones lurking in the back. No, I said, I was not a good person. Watch me in a business deal when I am after the best possible deal for my employees, my shareholders, my family, especially watch me if my family are threatened, then I am not a very nice person at all – and certainly not good. This they actually seemed to like, perhaps I had touched on the Russian soul itself.

It was shortly after that that Gorbachev allowed a few rubles to be used for paint for one of the few remaining Churches in Moscow. I attended the first service and was utterly amazed at the numbers as the Church/Cathedral was jam packed but the spirituality of the participants was beyond belief, especially as the practice of Christianity had been forbidden for 70 years. Incidentally services in the Russian Orthodox Church seem never ending!

My own belief again is simple and was probably shaped by my Aunts as a child. They were all most religious Church of England, Anglo Catholics, and always reminded me that it was 'high church'. I was taught that I should always pray, and if I did so, then my prayers would be answered, 'knock on any door and it shall be opened unto to you'. I think that I totally misunderstood the purpose, because each time that I was forbidden by my mother to do something, then I always went away, aged four or five, prayed fervently, and when I went back to my mother and asked again then she would always say 'yes, you can do that now'. So I assumed, at that young age, that that was all that was ever needed to get your own way !!!

I was also given a St Christopher medallion by my Aunt B and told that I would always be protected as St Christopher was the patron saint of travelers. At that age everything is very black and white, and I most firmly believed and adhered to whatever I was told. Also that I had a Guardian Angel who would always protect me. This I firmly believed, but if that was so then I have indeed most sorely tried their patience over the years.

What approach do I use in practice today? Simply 360 degree vision. Treat everything, no matter how odd it seems, with total acceptance and without astonishment. If I kick the bucket tomorrow, and end up in Hell, then they will probably have a sports club, which will no doubt have a tread mill which never stops, and a swimming pool where, once you start swimming lengths, then they go on forever. If it's Heaven then I will simply get a huge rocket for the way in which I have lived my life. If there's nothing, then it will not matter anyway, because I won't know about it !!

CHAPTER 5

Honour thy father and thy mother

Exedous 20:12

Do we always take after our parents? big question. Although our DNA, our genetic make up, and consequently our personality profiles are said not to alter, we can learn to accept and develop with what we have got, however it certainly took me an awful long while to learn the meaning of compromise. It could well be that medical science will shortly make this self induced learning process redundant as research scientists are working on the removal of certain inherited diseases (and no doubt traits) in the womb, but the ethics committees will no doubt have their say, and do have genuine concerns.

I was very fortunate in that although both my parents were working, I did have a support system with Aunts, Great Aunts, Uncles and extended family. My paternal grandfather was not among these having run off with a waitress when he was in his fifties. My father was very upset when he discovered that his parents were not married, but what I found even more hilarious was when the wife of one of my nephews friends, when we were all discovering the internet for genealogy, sent me an email with the message "we've found out why your grandparents were never married, it's because your grandfather was already married!"

Maybe I have a peculiar sense of humour, but I thought it funny, especially as I had the impression from a number of relations that perhaps my grandfather was from the wrong side of the blanket from a titled and distinguished family. I also wondered if this could be the case as early in my business career when, having been backed by some very wealthy merchant bankers, my backer said to me "You know we act for the Stanley family", I kept quiet and simply nodded as I hadn't a clue as to what he was referring. I was told many years later that he was probably talking about the Stanley's of Knowsley Hall and he was wondering if I was a 'plant'.

He need not have worried as when we did start on the family history we traced the line back to Standley's who were agricultural labourers in the 1700's in Norfolk, and who must have moved to London in search of work in the 1800's, as the first mention of my grandfather was in the census of 1881 when he was one of a very large household in what was then not exactly the most salubrious quarter of London. How on earth they all crammed into that small house I do not know, but he certainly did not let his environment hold him back. He left my grandmother with a house and support, my father with a business, and no doubt a few half brothers and sisters somewhere.

I met him when I had just left the army, he was extremely fit, well over 80 and died of a heart attack in his nineties when reputedly attempting to negotiate a new overdraft with his bank manager. From not the best of starts he did manage to become president of a number of sporting institutions, a successful business man, enough money to put my father through public school, and a very good sportsmen with a single figure golf handicap and a most respected member of the England Bowls team in the early twenties.

My father was the most gentle of men in all senses of the word, and a short while before his death he did ask me if there was anything that he possessed that I would like. Immediately I plumped for his book which he simply handed to me there and then. From this I discovered that he thought that his father was an absolute bastard, but this could have been because of the treatment handed out to my grandmother. For me that book was everything, it encompassed his entire life and was started when he was first sent away to school. Had I have read it earlier, and particularly in light of comments from my own son, who was also dispatched to boarding school at an early age, then I believe that I would probably have not sent either Roger or my daughter, Gaye, to board. I will, most probably, be in hot water for saying this, but having now almost reached my nineties I will do so anyway. Children need love before anything else, and this is best delivered by both parents – in my view at any rate !!

It is not quite accurate to say that my father's book encompassed his entire life as all writing ceased, somewhat abruptly, after the occasion when he parked his car on Pendine beach, went for a swim, and literally had to swim home when the car disappeared beneath the waves. He swam out too far and the tide came in too quickly.

On the maternal side my great, great grandfather was German and my great, great grandmother, French; they fled to England in the mid 1800's to avoid persecution. This was never discussed at all, especially during the war. Again my generation thought nothing of this as, having spent 3 years in Germany, I had learned just about enough German to order a glass of beer, my French was even worse, it was never given a second thought until my nephew, Charles, who distrusts all foreigners, remarked that we would have never been bombed during the war as we were family!

This probably makes us seem quite a mix except for the fact that all families are a mix if you go back far enough, but if you go all the way back (genetics again), we all come from the same stock. I often wonder why on earth we get into so many tribal/country/global disputes when we are all related, but on the other hand families get into real disputes anyway. Our Kings used to kill their sons quite frequently and if we think about it, if we do beat ourselves up, then it is no small wonder that we do fall out with others from time to time.

When I first visited the USA I loved the way everyone was so friendly, and everyone used to say "have a nice day"; that was until I realised that it was just a little "on top" and if they didn't like you, or if you annoyed them, then they wouldn't hesitate to take out a gun and shoot you. I really prefer someone who tells you exactly what they think, at least you do know where you stand.

So it does seem that there is a lot of suffering in the world, so who causes it? Is this too large a question, is it too complex? Not really, think about it, who causes us suffering? We do, we cause our own suffering. We cause our own suffering because of the way in which we view matters. Earlier I quoted Saeed Ansari, let me turn back to his words as he has a special and enlightened way of expressing certain situations. "Is this thought, this action, this person going to upset me, to cause me hurt? If so simply STOP and REFLECT. In most cases it is simply our own view of the proposed action that does the damage rather than the action itself". Or as we used to get taught as children "count to ten".

Here are Saeed's exact words on the subject:

"We should always be aware of our thoughts and feelings and bring ourselves to an an internal state of peace for our well-being and for the well-being of others. Why do we easily get hurt emotionally, and then react psychologically to ourselves in a destructive way? After all, anger is simply a waste of energy and the only person who is hurt is the person who becomes angry. We all need to learn to hold back from expressing our immediate, and at times extreme, emotional reaction. It would indeed be of considerable help were we to practice holding back from expressing such immediate emotion. Here are my five simple steps to help you restrain your destructive emotional reactions. Most of us are affected by our emotional experiences, and therefore I would like to suggest that you develop an extra ability, which is to **'Stop, breathe and reflect'**, so that it can help you handle and manage your emotional experiences rationally.

1. **Stop**.
2. **Breathe** rhythmically to gain clarity of mind.
3. **Reflect** calmly to gain insight.
4. **Take action** to complete your feelings with your new insight.
5. **Let go** of that which has been.

Go through the five steps to complete your feelings whenever you find yourself being emotionally reactive or emotionally disturbed. (Incomplete feelings give rise to anger, hatred, resentment, bitterness, revenge etc.) My suggestion is that you do the very best that you can to complete your feelings. Only completion of your feelings can make you feel happy. When you are mentally happy, you think better and you feel better. In other words you become creative, productive rather than destructive. Never leave your feelings incomplete, you will become aware that incomplete feelings make you resentful. For me it is much easier to complete my feelings, as well as much easier for me to change myself: changing myself, inwardly, saves me from all the pain as well as the chronic stress that goes with trying, mostly ineffectively, to change another person. For example: Let's suppose you are with a person, who has done something to upset you. You could stop and reflect to know what he did, what he is like and why he did it, or you could go into what you are like, and how it upsets you. And if you go into yourself, this would be a great revelation for you. 'Stop, breathe and reflect' is a necessary process for you to go through in order to think rationally and to focus on the positive. Otherwise, without the use of 'Stop, breathe and reflect', you will be hurting yourself with your own negative thinking, and very likely to continue to hurt yourself with it until it is resolved either within your own mind or within the other person.

'Stop, breathe and reflect' is a powerful tool which makes you realise that 'the cause of your problem lies within you and not outside of you'. So look for the cause in yourself: There is a great deal to learn from the sage Confucius who taught: "If an archer misses the target, he finds no fault with the target, nor with the bow, nor with the arrow, but with himself alone". So, you too can act in this manner, locating the root cause of your emotional upsets or the cause of your anger in your own self. I also believe that a great change in our psychological attitude is necessary. We need more understanding of our psychological world, because psychologically, we humans have not changed very much. We are still barbaric, killing each other, cannot tolerate this person, cannot tolerate that person etc. Psychologically, we tend to live in misery and confusion at times......and are pitifully unaware of all this. So therefore please do master this secret; if someone is angry with you, don't be angry yourself."

Saeed is extremely gifted in such matters, and is highly respected within the Bristol community as he is someone who always practices what he 'preaches'. Preach is probably the wrong word as he simply lives a life based on help for others. And this he does with simplicity.

CHAPTER 6

The beginning is a good place to start

From little Acorns mighty Oak trees grow

Earlier I mentioned upbringing so how did I set about putting my first hesitant steps on to the planet? Well I chose the right parents who were able to let me have a broad upbringing. They had a business, Ealing Common Nurseries, which occupied them for long periods of time except for when my father was undertaking his film work, mainly the old Denham studios, also when they were not playing some sport or other. They were the ladies and men's singles champions respectively at their tennis club in Acton when they got married.

This meant that, as I had a number of relations who also had business's, a considerable number of my relations would take it in turns to look after - and educate me – when my parents, Bob and Bits, were not around. This was indeed a broad education as we had a family laundry in Acton; Acton had so many laundries that at one time it was known as 'soapsuds island', and so my business education commenced at a very early age. My Great Aunt Kate used to take me round all the 'ironers' when she would note down how many garments had been ironed, I think that it was a farthing a garment. This would all be entered in separate books later to be transcribed to ' the ledger'. Hence my introduction to costing at the age of three.

There was also Aunt B, who I learnt many years later had apparently, according to my mother, been a missionary in Belize: I still have the St Christopher medallion that she gave me over eighty years ago. She and Aunt Kate were a wonderful, good guy, bad guy, act. Aunt Kate super efficient and workaholic, Aunt B compassion personified. I also had two uncles, Dick and Derrick, again absolute opposites as were my Aunt Da and her sister, my mother, Bits. Da (she was actually Frieda but I couldn't pronounce that when I was younger so it got shortened to 'Da') looked after me for much of the time when I was younger.

Was this an idyllic childhood? – for me, yes but, and it is a big but – it suited me. I am fully aware that it was not a text book upbringing, and would not have suited the vast majority of people reading and who have read so far. I had access to different personalities, different views, but not that much contact with my actual parents, no access to other children, the money making side came before anything else. I think that I was about three or four years old when my parents, Bob and Bits, invited some neighbours children in for a party. I ran away and hid – I'd never seen other children !

My mother would always belt the living daylights out of me but was always fiercely protective of me to outsiders. I rarely saw my father who always used to say that children should be born at three years old. When I was much older, Da, who was the maiden aunt, and in those days maiden aunts performed the 'child care' duties in the family, told me, after she was eventually married, that I was a mistake and not wanted. None of this mattered a jot. I loved both my parents equally, always did, always will do and totally venerate their memory. I appreciate the love, most undemonstrative love by the way, that they showed *in their own way* for Penny and myself. Love comes in many forms and sometimes that old maxim of being cruel to be kind can apply. I'll wait for the shouts from you all on that one !!!

These were the years immediately preceding the outbreak of war. During the war my parents moved heaven and earth to look after me, and later Penny who was not born until 1942. As you get older your memories reduce, years get squashed together, compressed, so that events that happened thirty years ago can appear, in your mind, to have happened at the same time as those sixty years ago.

One very clear memory is that of my aunts talking with my mother on the day that war was declared on the 3rd September 1939. I can still experience the depth of the concern that permeated all possible sensations at the time. I was six years old, did not understand what was being said, but I do remember the atmosphere, the unsettling worry, and the disquiet. But only on that one occasion, not even the time when the London docks were ablaze for a week before the government admitted on the radio that they had actually been hit. However you could not mistake the fierce glow that lit up the night skies for the whole of that period. The family comment was "that didn't look too good" and then they simply got on with the task of daily living as best they could.

The only time that I saw real concern was when an incendiary bomb fell in our family laundry's little courtyard. No fridges in those days so food was stored in the 'meat safe,' which was an open wooden container covered in a very fine zinc gauze mesh which allowed air in but hopefully, nothing else. The incendiary bomb came down right next to the safe, but did not explode and was still smoldering. My aunt rushed outside, opened the safe door and gathered up a plate with something wrapped in fine muslin. She then hurtled back indoors where my uncles were horrified, they then rushed out with buckets of sand and stirrup pumps to douse the now very unstable looking incendiary bomb. When they thought that they had got the bomb finally immobilised, they came back in and asked my aunt what on earth she thought that she was doing by taking such a risk. "I was very worried" she said "that was our whole weeks meat ration in that safe, I couldn't possibly allow it to be lost in that way just because of a stupid German bomb!!"

I can never remember being the slightest bit hungry, despite the rationing, nor was I ever perturbed in any way. Possibly that's an age thing combined with the protection given to children in the war years. Of course it also depends upon what attitudes are adopted by those around you; certainly you were taught never to waste food, and to always eat whatever was in front of you. As certain foods were impossible to obtain you developed a liking for their substitutes. I still hanker after reconstituted eggs, dried egg or was it simply called, powdered egg?. Whale meat tasted just like steak, but I have heard that other people found it totally inedible.

Because most of the men were away fighting at the front I credit the ladies for a having had a very happy childhood, despite the war years; they were always cheerful, always protective, and always sharing whatever little that they possessed; I recently discovered fascinating letters between aunts and great aunts "I have put a postal order for 2/6p (two shillings and sixpence in old money) in the post and hope that this will help". Others, "I have posted the dirty washing, could you return the blouse as soon as possible please as I have only the two". Make do and mend certainly applied!

You made your own amusements, but the great thing was to collect shrapnel. I had a wonderful cat called Lionel. He had a huge mane and looked just like a lion, every time the Air Raid siren sounded signaling the start of an air raid he would come tearing into the house, jump on my chest and stay there until the 'all clear' sounded. Then he would jump off so that I could get up and sneak off to collect shrapnel.

I would carefully climb out of my bedroom window on to a very narrow wooden ledge (below me was a glass roof !), cling on to the wall, and edge my way on to the flat roof of the laundry next door. If it had been a heavy raid there was always plenty of shrapnel from the German bombs and our shells, not to mention the incendiary's. I still have some of that collection, but had I been caught by my mother, or by one of my aunts, then I would not be alive to tell the tale. Neither would I have been had I lost my footing and gone through the glass roof. As I mentioned earlier, at a very young age my great aunt insisted that I had a 'guardian angel', and so would come to no harm. If that was the case then they must have been the most overworked angel in the whole of creation!! I was either entirely dependent upon that Guardian Angel or just plain stupid! - or very lucky!!!

Wars are never sensible, cut out the ego and wars would not exist but sometimes, with deep regret, they happen, period. But like everything else they come to an end. Do we learn from them? Possibly, but we do not seem to take any real preventative action, and although no global war has erupted since 1945, the regional conflicts have threatened total mayhem. Having spent a considerable time in Russia, I would like to sling in my take on what is now the current conflict in Ukraine, especially on absolute power corrupting absolutely, but I will leave that until later. Solution for all this, haven't got one, sorry.

So how did Bits, my mother, and Bob, my father, cope? How did all the other members of my family, and my extended family manage during those war years? Simple, acceptance. There is no other way. If you want to delve into this further read some Russian authors, read Solshetizin's 'Gulag Archipelago', or his arresting 'One Day in the Life of Ivan Denisovich' or better still read Boris Pasternak's 'Doctor Zhivago'. However a simpler way is to see the film, not so many pages or complicated plots, but the film is a bit long though. It also is a brilliant lesson in humanity − also please do read Anna Pasternak's book 'Lara', wonderful definition of human frailty, and the true meaning of love; if you are not aware of it, this is the true story upon which Doctor Zhivago is based, and is the fascinating story of Boris Pasternak's life or at least his somewhat complicated love life.

Pre war, Bob and Bits enjoyed a great life, Bob had his film work with the likes of George Formby, and stage work with Ivor Novello. He was forever auditioning for new parts, and was very good on the dance side as he used to have a dance act with a partner when he was sent to Australia as a young man by his father, the reason for which has never been disclosed; he obviously got fed up with the sheep farming and took various jobs, one of which was as a taxi driver in Sydney, so when not performing his dance routine he would have some sort of income. He was always complaining that if ever he got to speak a few lines filming in the UK, then that scene would always end up on the cutting room floor! However he and Bits also had the Ealing Common

Nurseries, who were described as 'Court Florists', but as they also had an excellent manager, they were able to continue being the tennis stars of the Springfield Acton Bowling Club where George Stanley, Bob's father, had been President.

War comes along, Bob volunteers for the RAF, but the queue was too long so he joined the Army which was a much shorter queue. Impatience must be genetic. We all used to live in a lovely house in Acton with Bob's mother Lydia, however I always called her Nanna. The house had been bequeathed to her by Bob's father George, who by this time had shot off with his lady friend leaving Nanna with the house, and Bob with the business.

After the outbreak of hostilities and his initial training, Bob was posted to an anti-aircraft site in Norfolk, Bits promptly followed, so the house was requisitioned and Nanna went to live in a bed sit around the corner. They never did get the house back, the nurseries got bombed and had to shut anyway, not much need for flower arranging in war time. I never heard anyone complain though, they just got on with daily living, survival was the motivation, but as I said earlier, I was never hungry and never unhappy. I had that wonderful cat who as I mentioned previously, would always come dashing in and lay on my chest when the air raid sirens sounded the alert for a raid and would never leave until the all clear was sounded. He got injured and had to be taken to the vets in a push chair. I can remember the awful wait at the vets, and the door opening but no Lionel, they had to have him put down. I simply bawled my eyes out, and could not be stopped despite being placed in the push chair and wheeled all the way home – and I must have been around nine at the time!

Bob was posted overseas and went all along the North African coast with the eighth army and then up through Italy. We hadn't seen him for some three or four years so when he did return, the dashing young man who went to war seemed to have returned aged beyond recognition. We were then living with other family members at the laundry at 116 Avenue Road in Acton, so when I opened the door to him I can still remember my total astonishment at the change. He must have felt the same.

CHAPTER 7

Grumpy old man

When we learn to accept and love, every aspect of our life begins to thrive
- Daaji

So why the weird title for this chapter? These events took place over seventy years ago and were during the post war years so everyone used to just get on with things, the rationing, shortages, housing deprivation, clothes coupons, demob suits to name but a few, so when people of my generation hear whinges from people of a younger age today, they do produce a somewhat wry smile from us. We learned to make do and mend, waste nothing, throw nothing away (in joke simply put in for my son Roger!). People moan, mourn, complain and expect the world to sort everything out for them today. We got taught self sufficiency with heavy handed discipline, and in my opinion it certainly provided a wonderful platform for life, especially resilience! OK I'll get off that soap box as by now I will have lost at least three generations of readers!!

Or possibly not. All generations moan about the previous generation and the generations that are to come. I have found that the generation of teenagers today are exceptionally kind, thoughtful and bubbly, not a single suggestion that they have been handed a 'bum steer' with climate change, political chaos and a ruling elite more concerned with not upsetting anyone by placating any and every so called minority group. Uh oh, another two generations of readers about to disappear.

Housing, jobs, education, were real problems and it is with exceptional gratitude that I think back to those times when we had to move, move again, and constantly concern ourselves, or at least my parents did, with daily living. We eventually settled in Iselworth in a flat previously occupied by my uncle Derrick, who was himself recently demobbed, but he needed to live in the accommodation at the laundry in Acton as, being the eldest son, he took over the running and responsibility for the operation. This did not please my uncle Dick who had been undertaking this duty in Derrick's absence during the war. Dick could not serve in the forces because of his eyes and general health.

Both were cycling enthusiast to the highest degree, and they educated me in all matters relating to the sport, but one day fell out over the laundry. They had a right old punch up and I can remember to this day, mopping all the blood up afterwards. It was, though, an utterly invaluable lesson as to the stupidity of ownership and possessions, the false value of money and the total need for family unity, but stress does very funny things as I was later to find out, especially if you are in the position of leadership, and your decisions can make or break people.

Bits, Penny and I decamped to the ground floor flat previously occupied by Derrick and his family in Hexham Gardens, Isleworth, accommodation really was very difficult and in short supply in those days shortly after the war end. I always remember Bob's mother, my grandmother Lydia who was called 'Nanna' living in that tiny little bed sit just around the corner from her own beautiful house. Requisitioning during the war produced many iniquities. She never received any compensation but was always exceptionally stoic about that, and everything else, you had to be, it's called acceptance, and is indeed a most valuable trait.

Bits moved heaven and earth to get me what she described as decent schooling, and I ended up at the Gunnersbury Catholic Grammar School, which was just on the edge of the old Rothchild family residence at Gunnersbury Park, which the Rothchild's gifted to the nation. Penny attended the local Isleworth primary school, and I used to take Penny on adventure travels, just hopping on a bus on a Saturday morning and bagging the front seat on the top deck. When sweets were taken off the ration book, or rather when the allowance was increased, we descended on the local sweet shop and carried home armfuls, we have both retained a propensity for devouring the wretched calorie infused delicacies ever since. However I cannot remember ever seeing anyone who was other than 'slim', obesity was unknown in those day.

OK, what about the relation of all this to well being? Well it's all about resilience and acceptance, both essential ingredients for well being but what about the others? Let's cover belief systems, meditation, exercise and nutrition as aids to developing the right attitude of mind later on, and in the next chapter, look at some reasons why the right attitude can really assist, as it may be a good juncture to examine how attitude of mind can help in those situations that always seem to crop up when least expected. Specifically how it has helped me even as I write this book.

CHAPTER 8

Life's a shit – so what – deal with it

We cannot always do great things but we can
always do small things with great love

I started to write this chapter at the time the events happened and have not revisited it until now, so I trust that you will excuse the apparent time lapses.

Well now I can start practicing what I was preaching just a few pages back. Two weeks ago my son Roger rang me to tell me that he had to cancel a visit to us as his wife, Ruth, had pains in her stomach. Having got home from the hospital that evening he rang to let us know what was wrong "Dad, Ruth has pancreatic cancer", "that's not so good" I said. "No" he replied "It's too far advanced and has spread, and they have only given her another four months".

So what do you do, and what do you say? What is more important, what will Ruth do and how best can we help and support her and our son Roger, in this situation? Everyone has their own reaction, there is no right or wrong approach in these circumstances, we are all different, and we all cope in our own unique and individual ways.

Ruth's reaction was brilliant, she went with some of her friends to a 'Take That' concert in Manchester, then she did some ironing, painted the kitchen, and finally went with Roger to a friends birthday party in Berlin! Of course this is all in between constant medical appointments and discussions in order to find the correct combination of drugs just to keep the pain down, then the visits to oncologists, MDT (Multi Disciplinary Teams), specialist hospitals, and subsequent visits from the Macmillan nurses who were, and have always been, utterly brilliant.

I rang my sister, Penny, to let her know and found out that my brother in law, Don, had developed acute myeloid leukemia! It was at this point that I had to stop beating myself up for writing those few pages back about my mother curing her cancer, and putting that paragraph in the second chapter about the well balanced people who tread a middle path and a thundering great truck comes along and catches them treading a path in the middle of the road! Just a little too prophetic!

Don is just off for his chemo, but he can only have doses sufficient to improve his quality of life, not curative as is the case with my daughter in law, Ruth, but that is because her cancer is too far advanced for anything else to be of any use at all. In some ways though he is very fortunate as he can only have, at his age, mild doses of chemo whereas Ruth will be given maximum strength. Neither are funny and the only thing that Mame and I can do to help is to be there when needed, but the heavier doses of chemo are not at all pleasant.

It is now two weeks later and again, my bloody stupid prophetic writing, I really do think that I will have to stop writing this book. They have given Ruth her chemo, and she is now in Clatterbridge which is a center of excellence in the Wirral for the treatment of cancer: there were severe complications following her first dose of chemo and they are desperately trying to keep the pain down, but at the same time get some form of sustenance into her body as she could not eat, and certainly could not keep anything down. Roger has performed miracles in care since Ruth was first diagnosed, and so have all the other cancer carers and help organisations, Macmillan's, Pancreatic Cancer Society, Cancer Research UK, and many others who give tireless support to help so many people, as they did when I had my little bout of cancer but that's for later, let me get back to where we were. So when did I first believe that suffering was a load of nonsense and try to do something about it? When I was very small............

Let me come back to that later as well. Ruth died almost four months to the day that she was first diagnosed. Her funeral was last week. Roger's care and compassion were not just exemplary but outstanding, and he was with her right to the end in the Severn Hospice, which is just a short way outside Shrewsbury. Ruth's acceptance, care and compassion for others, her total lack of any question of self pity are far best summed up by Roger in his eulogy.

Roger did also state in his eulogy of Ruth's total lack of concern for herself, her practicality and her thought for others. Kubler Ross, well known in psychiatric circles for her detailed pronouncements on bereavement (not everyone agrees with her, however you will always have disagreement in academic environments, which is good as reality or truth is very much akin to shifting sands) categorised the following states in bereavement: Denial, Isolation, Anger, Bargaining, Depression and finally Acceptance. These states do not all necessarily happen and can be gone through, and gone back to, again and again. But in the end there does need to be acceptance.

As a family we are exceptionally fortunate in that the only state that we ever saw in Ruth was absolute acceptance, and the same from Roger. As I mentioned earlier acceptance is a wonderful gift and Ruth's acceptance and willingness to discuss this was of considerable help to all of us. However she did make one request of me and that was to ensure that Roger was OK after she had gone. As she also asked Mame I have no doubt whatsoever that she also asked other friends and family. I will honour that until I am no longer around, and even then I will be keeping an eye on it.

CHAPTER 9

Belief Systems

This is my simple religion, there is no need for complicated philosophy, our own brain, our own heart is our temple, the philosophy is kindness.
- HH The Dali Lama

Let's get back to the well being side. Why do I believe in belief systems? Because they do you good - how? As a tremendous back up for your immune system. What do I do if I am really ill? I go to bed, pull the curtains and sleep. I leave the rest to sleep and to my immune system, and all those others who are usually dependent on me, the microbes, the bacteria, the mitochondria, the telemores, the cells, the protons, the neurons and all the others to which my body is host.

Why do I take so many multi vitamin pills and so many herbal products, until the price is too great when I then immediately drop them? Because I believe that they do me good. I believe that they do me good and so I benefit from that belief, it is the belief that does me far more good than whatever pills or medicines that I may take. What clinical trials can I quote to back this up – none at all, but I certainly have a considerable number of medical friends who tell me that I am right. Take probiotics ; I understand that at the best they do you no harm but I am constantly being told that it is pretty useless sticking 5 billion or 10 billion 'good' bacteria into your gut when your gut has hundreds of billions of other strains of 'good' bacteria, and what I am doing is just a drop in the ocean anyway.

However I do think that they should be used if you are taking antibiotics as these drugs are used to kill the 'bad' bacteria, but also have a catastrophic effect on the 'good' bacteria. They are a little indiscriminate. Another reason why I think that we depend far too much on drugs to cure. They cost a fortune. Far better to spend the money on prevention. Yes, I'll get off that soap box!

Dr. Lisa Rankin, who gives super TED talks, specifically highlights the power of belief systems in her book 'Mind Over Medicine'. Basically the brain responds to positive beliefs by releasing chemicals that put the body in a state of of physiological rest. Under this condition the body is primarily controlled by the parasympathetic nervous system, but negative beliefs trigger the stress response, and the cellular system gets poisoned with stress hormones.

So are all belief systems inherently good? Sorry but I'm afraid not; in the wrong hands they can be used to manipulate the unwary, the spiritual seeker, the spiritual butterfly (those that continually flit from one sect or religious belief to another), the mentally troubled, and the genuine seeker. History is littered with those who have abused their powers, and that does not exclude the main stream religions. How about the Spanish Inquisition, the burning of witches, but look what happens in the end. Before the recent abuse scandals in Ireland, the Catholic Church used to exert their influence over some 80% of the population. This has now dropped to around 40% a decade later. Regrettably the abused are still suffering and still continually beat themselves up.

Aleister Crowley, who was notorious as 'The Beast' or '666', started off as a sincere practitioner of Yoga, the Maharishi in the USA, who ended up with a string of Rolls Royce and even more mistresses, and the really bad ones such as Manson who caused multiple deaths. As you will gather, I am not in favour of cults! Mame and I once attended a highly marketed sales conference, yes, these can also be classed as belief systems, and to encourage us we were flown over to Nice where the very intelligent audience were transfixed. Mame was superb, she simply stood up and marched out, I followed. The main guy eventually got put away for fraud, but not before a whole lot of people lost a whole lot of money – and their dignity.

I do not think that any of us is strong enough to totally resist persistent manipulation or brainwashing especially if you are deprived of sleep. Again another story. What about those people, such as Richard Dawkins who put forward the most logical thesis for the no God argument, who are utterly sincere in their belief of their own conclusions. Well that is exactly the point, it is their belief, their BELIEF system. So how about this then, a no belief, belief system – what on earth is that ???

Have no attachment to any belief system, does it matter if you are right or wrong, do you have to be right or wrong anyway? Many think of Buddhism as one of the worlds most rapidly growing religions but it isn't actually a religion, there is no God, it is really a philosophy, a physiological or psychological system, a method of training the mind. The mind eventually comes to have no attachment to anything, to any belief, to any object, to any person and finally, to life itself. This does not mean that you cannot love someone, quite the opposite, but it is with unconditional love rather than selfish love – no attachment. As for life itself, does it really matter, it is all about how you have lived your life, your consideration for others, not for how well you have done or how long you have lived.

The one thing that I have never done in my life is to have died, so that is why I am really looking forward to it as it must be classed as a one off ! My Buddhist and Hindu friends tell me that I must have lived many lives, but advancing years and memory probably take their toll because I have no recollection of such matters at all !

CHAPTER 10

School - the happiest days of your life – why?

Let us remember that one book, one pen and one teacher can change the world - Malala Yousafzai

So what was school really like for me? I used to miss substantial portions of lessons though illness, and once, having spent most of a couple of terms either in hospital or in bed at home, the headmaster wanted me to drop back a year in order to catch up as I had missed so many lessons. My mother was having none of it, she insisted that I stayed up with my allotted year, but what she did not realise was that I had missed too much and could not follow what I was then being taught. So when I did get back to school, I went from being one of the bright ones to just plain stupid, so I then got ridiculed for my lack of knowledge. I always call this the 'wounded seagull' syndrome, you get attacked if you are different from the rest of the herd. As seagulls will do to any gull who appears 'different'.

This really was a blessing in disguise as I started to miss the academic lessons, I think that it is called exclusion these days, and so I was able to start playing sport. What a benefit this was, especially for my well-being side, I cycled, swam and went cross country running, got taught table tennis by a wonderful school friend who would spend hours with me showing me how to perfect different shots, he was a natural but I was only able to become proficient by constant practice, practice, practice.

As I progressed my sports master decreed that I could not cycle, swim and run as they were three different sports and each sport used a different set of muscles, so I would have to concentrate on just one sport: triathlons had not yet been invented!! I perfected my swimming, became the school swimming captain but then we all moved from Isleworth to South Wales as Bob, my father, was appointed adjutant at the School of Artillery at Manorbier in Pembrokeshire.

Wow! Gunnersbury Grammar in Acton was boys only but Pembroke Dock Grammar School was co-ed, I was just reaching that in between age and thought that I'd arrived in heaven! It was here that I met the first love of my life but I'm leaving out anything else about that little episode until book 3.Incidentally book 1, which is what you are currently reading, is basically a well-being memoir; book 2 is all about work, the city, the mafia, the establishment, but book 3 will be a beautiful love story. Anyway there was only one swimming pool in the whole of the county of Pembrokeshire, outdoors at that, so I swapped my swimming for running and ended up representing Pembrokeshire schoolboys for the mile.

That change did lead to, not the first, nor for that matter my last, episode of sheer stupidity, simply yet another piece of act first, think later; which is why that I can now look back, with much gratitude, to that 'Guardian Angel'. Fools rushing in where angels fear to tread must be my motto. I was a little older at this time, it was shortly after the war had finished, not too long after we had moved to Pembrokeshire, and we were living close to the sea, actually about seven miles which was either walked or cycled. I challenged the local swimming champion to a race. I should win, I had swum in a real swimming bath, most people in Pembroke either used the mill pond or the sea. Also I had been the school swimming captain, what is that about pride coming before a fall?

The local champion was older and wiser, said that the challenge should be to swim out to sea and the first to give up would lose the race. It must have been six to seven hundred yards to get out of the bay and into the open sea, but out beyond the headland the waves became larger. I had swallowed too much water, you don't get waves in swimming baths. I indicated that I ought to go back, and we both set off in return, somewhat difficult as the tide had other ideas. I was exceptionally tired but my companion constantly urged me not to give up, he was used to these waters and realised the danger.

We could not swim directly towards the beach because the wind was against us and the tide was sweeping us towards the rocks on the right hand side of the bay. That's right hand looking towards the beach from the sea. I kept saying, in between mouthfuls of salty water, "let the tide take us, we can rest on the rocks", again my companion, very, very wisely was having none of it, he knew the danger as we would have been battered trying to climb out of the sea on to the rocks, let alone the cold had we actually been able to clamber out. We could not have been more than two hundred yards from the shore but the next thing I remembered was the crowd all around me,

"We thought he was dead"

"Couldn't stop him swimming, he swam all the way up the beach, his arms and legs were still going but his eyes were shut"

"Miracle he's still alive"

"Ought to know better with these tides"

I owed my life to my companion that day, apparently I had been unconscious for over an hour, and the biggest problem that the people on the beach had was to stop my arms and legs moving because, although unconscious, I still went on swimming automatically. Now I couldn't recall my companion/opponents name but, yes, I did owe him my life.

As for stupid acts let me trot out yet another, canoeing! I was living in North London having recently ended my tour of duty in the Army and I wanted a trip abroad but couldn't afford it as I was studying to be an accountant and the remuneration was minuscule, however I loved canoeing, in fact my folding canoe went everywhere with me. I would take it on the bus from my little bed sit in North London, assemble it when I got to the banks of the Thames, and then canoe to my firms highly respected clients. That was until I canoed from Tower Bridge to a Rickett

Cockerell coal depot near Greenwich, left it on their wharf, went to go home in the evening and found it full of coal dust. That was the last time that I ever did that!

This time I took it to Dover on the bus, assembled it on the beach, and set off with a little pocket compass and a packet of sandwiches. I paddled out from the main port entrance, got hailed by the authorities who wanted to know the name of my vessel. Bet that was the first time that they had had to register a canoe as a maritime vessel. I made up some name and paddled onward.

On a clear day you can see the coast of France from the cliffs at Dover, but not when you are at sea level and sat in a canoe. After three hours I didn't know where I was, the waves were getting bigger but I didn't dare let the canoe capsize as I hadn't got a life jacket, didn't get a weather forecast before setting off, and had not informed the coast guards. Very, very stupid. A small sea going freighter was passing in front of me with a somewhat bemused look out, so I hailed him and asked the direction of Calais. The lookout pointed to a totally different direction to that in which I was heading. That couldn't be right I thought, so continued onward, but now it was getting dark. I was getting more and more anxious until I spotted some lights on the horizon, paddled furiously, and eventually finished up on the beach at Sangatte, and that wasn't Calais! Maybe that look out on that freighter had been right all along.

As I couldn't speak much French I indicated to the somewhat bemused French onlookers, who appeared from nowhere when I had staggered out of the canoe, that I needed somewhere to sleep for the night. That certainly proved that my French was next to useless, but then my sign language was even worse, as they took me to the local brothel! Eventually they found me a bed for the night in a small hotel, and after a hearty breakfast I decided that I would rather catch the ferry home. This time some common sense did prevail. Perhaps it might have been better if I had concentrated a little harder on lessons in school rather than the sports!!!

School for me was a great place of learning, not so much in the academic field but in learning about that 'flow' that Helen mentioned in her introduction, I just had fun. Whichever sport in which I was a participant, I concentrated on with the uttermost dedication at that very moment, I also learned about success, but more especially, about failure. Failing possibly teaches you much more than success.

Somehow or other I did not seem to play much soccer or cricket, possibly because I fell in love with rugger and made the 1st XV, and represented the county at athletics. I had learnt my tennis by first knocking a ball against a wall whilst we were still at Isleworth, and that became my main sport. When I first started knocking up against a wall I used my fathers old per-war, wooden framed racquet, but Bob did say that he would buy me a proper new racquet, but only once I had won my first tournament.

There was no coaching in those days, so we had to learn amongst ourselves as tennis was not taught in school. I was about sixteen when I managed to get into the final of the Pembroke Dock Junior Open Tennis Tournament. I marched on to the court with this old and somewhat misshapen square headed wooden racquet which instead of going 'ping' sounded a very dull thud when connecting with a ball; then my opponent came on with six tournament strung, very modern racquets! As juniors we used to be lucky if we got on to a court, and I had never seen anyone watching any match, so I was totally amazed as there was quite a large crowd when we got on the court for the final. It turned out that my opponent was a certain Michael Davis who went on to have a very distinguished career as a professional tennis player and ended up as chairman of the World Professional Tennis Players Association, needless to say I lost!! However Bob did say that I had done well enough to warrant a modern racquet which he then duly bought for me.

I certainly have a tremendous amount of gratitude towards the game of tennis, it became the bedrock of Mame's and my partnership, our marriage and our life together. As Bob and Bits had been the singles champions at the Springfield Acton

Bowling and Tennis Club when they got married, Mame and I emulated them as we were ladies and gents singles champions at the Bethune Lawn Tennis club when we got married. We went on to play in a number of tournaments and were regulars in the Hertfordshire league for our club after we were married, which I think was named the Broxbourne Lawn Tennis club , I know that it boasted nine grass courts apart from their hard courts. In those days you could not join, you had to be 'played in' but I do not think that this is obligatory today.

So what about the academic side? Yes, well, er, that's about it. I was far too busy discovering girls and playing all the sports that were available. I did manage to get the school leaving certificate, GCSE these days, with credits in math and a couple of other subjects, one of which was English literature, which was hilarious as I had not even opened the book which had to be studied for the exam. One of the exam questions was describe a snow scene from the book; I simply let my imagination fly, made it all up and got a credit!! I did say at the start of this please, do NOT copy what I did !!

Also do not copy my stupid obsession for jumping in to help people. One day outside the school gates, shortly after I had arrived in Pembroke Dock, I saw a boy in the form below me in an argument with a much larger boy from the Coronation School, also in Pembroke Dock. I went over, "don't pick on someone smaller than you, if you want a fight then I'm here", I told the larger boy, got in between the two of them and squared up to him. All of a sudden the boy who I was trying to protect jumped on my back and started pummeling me. "What are you doing" I said "I'm trying to protect you", now having to fight the two of them, "he's my brother" said the younger boy. One day I will learn, perhaps.

Or perhaps not. When we were living in Isleworth I started a friendship with two boys some years older than myself, and it was not long before I realised that something wasn't right, they were using me to get into friends houses, play cards with my friends parents and cheat them at cards for money. They exerted control over me both psychologically and physically, and eventually tried it on in with Bits, my mother, in my own home and for money again. When we got outside I simply went for them, fists flailing furiously and with some inner strength that seemed to overcome height, reach and common sense. Luckily I went for the one who was only some three or four years older than me and had not the oldest one pulled me off him then I would have killed him. They went off, battered and bruised and I never saw them again. That was a lesson that I carry with me to this day, be honest, have integrity, and when you have no alternative, stand up for what you believe no matter what the cost.

Talking of costs, I also learned another invaluable lesson whilst living at Hexham Gardens in Isleworth. Money was always in very short supply, as was everything else after the war. I never threw anything away, especially my old comics, so I started races around the roads and gave the comics away as prizes, but charged each participant one penny to enter. This was quite a successful venture, but I was rapidly running out of comics to give as prizes, so I entered myself in each race and just had to win, otherwise there would have been no prizes to give. As I became more determined, and started to win every race, the other participants refused to enter. What did this teach me? Always have a plan B and don't over egg it.

The incident with the two bullies, which taught me how to use my fists, and the races which taught me never to give up, came in as extremely useful after we had moved to Pembrokeshire. Each year a visiting fair used to pitch up all along the high street in Pembroke, and probably still does for all I know, but they used to have a boxing booth and we all used to watch the challenges being thrown out nightly by the booth's professional boxers. There were always warm up fights between Pembroke residents before the main events, and one night one of the gypsy boys challenged me. As you got five shillings for this warm up fight, just three rounds, five shillings being the equivalent of ten weeks pocket money, I jumped at the chance as it wasn't just the five shillings but the 'nobbins', those are the coins that were thrown into the ring if you put up a good display. I was very lucky as my hands were held aloft at the end of the fight, and that started my apprenticeship with the 'pros' at the booth; they were so helpful, changing my style from southpaw to orthodox, and always finding time, in between their own fights, to coach and to encourage me. They taught me how to avoid serious injury, and although I lost fights as well as won them, I was never, ever, in any of my bouts actually knocked down.

What else did I learn during my school years? Well for a start, the true value of friendship and the true essence of leadership. When I first went to Pembroke Dock Grammar I met one, Joey Griffiths who led a gang, the 'McGregors', a most interesting number of local teenagers of school age, and what an inspirational leader he was, but who sadly died a few years ago. On my first entering the school we immediately struck up what was to become a life long friendship, he would always look after the weakest members of his gang and always ensure total fairness, if we took on another gang smaller than us we would always ask them to select one person from their gang, and to select one person from our gang. Then the two would do battle, and after the fight between the two people, not the whole gang, we would all shake hands. Again, doesn't happen today, does it?

When caught by the local policeman for such escapades as 'scrumping', that is stealing apples from orchards, the police would always give you an option, take a beating there and then, or be carted off to your home and your parents informed. We always took the beating. In many instances some of us would find ourselves playing alongside the same policeman in a rugger match on a Saturday morning, never a moment of animosity, if you got into an argument you settled it there and then, you never held a grudge.

Joey was a giant of a boy with a mane of blond hair always flying in the wind. One day for a laugh we challenged the rest of the school to try to get into the toilets and we would try to stop them by wedging ourselves in the doorway, no one got through, and we all had a huge laugh afterwards until a rather pretty prefect, June Strachan if I remember correctly, remonstrated with us, Joey walked off, but I argued the point, loser, well it was me – detention !!

CHAPTER 11

School to Army

Marching on !!

My first serious girl friend and I were very, very keen on each other but there were obstacles, Mary's father, a most fervent supporter of Welsh rule, disliked the English, intensely disliked the British Army, of which my father was a member, and thought that someone like myself should be shot on sight. My mother was exactly the opposite and concocted various pieces of cover in order that we could meet. Quite often matters went awry such as the night that I took a tent, couldn't erect it, so Mary and I simply snuggled down under the awnings and woke up in the morning in the local park, only to then find that we were covered in something like six inches inches of snow, try explaining that away !!

One day we concocted a story that Mary would visit one of her relations in North London, and at the same time I would visit my Aunt Da who lived in South Harrow. When asked by my Aunt as to the cover story, I said that I had told everyone that I was coming up to London to look for a job. "Right" she said, "you never lie so here is the Daily Telegraph, here is the jobs section, so get some applications off before you go to meet Mary". That's how I became an accountant as one of the replies was from E N Mason and Sons, Chartered Accountants of Buckingham Palace Gate.

What a brilliant first job, Masons were Brewery Auditors and audited all the major breweries. At 10.30 a.m every day, instead of being brought coffee, a crate of the breweries best beer arrived, I cannot ever remember being sober !! You got paid very little and as it was shortly after the end of the war, money was in very shot supply in our family. My father gave me a £5 note to cover my first weeks lodgings, but I blew most of that by taking my first love, Mary, for one last super night out in Tenby before I left Pembroke Dock for the bright lights of London.

I had enough left for the train fare but not for lodgings, so I used to sleep on Paddington station where you could get a bath for a shilling, and the hot water would keep you warm all night. My lovely Aunt Jill, and her husband Dick, took pity on me and put me up for a few weeks in their flat in Larden Road in Acton, and then my Aunt Da completed the family assistance by offering me a room at their house at 25 Torrington Drive, South Harrow.

My father had remained in the Army as he wanted me to go to Sandhurst, however I applied to the Fleet Air Arm as I wanted to fly jets off aircraft carriers, the reason being that you received £1500 at the end of your short service commission. I passed all the tests with literally flying colours, but the medical board would not pass me as some of those childhood illnesses showed up, especially sinus problems which still beset me to this day. They sent me all over Harley Street and goodness knows where else, but it was to no avail, no way could I fly jets off carriers said the medical establishment. I was probably quite lucky in a way as most of my intake failed to make it to collect the £1500, it turned out that flying jets off carriers had a somewhat high death rate!

This was the era when all 18 year olds were subject to call up for National Service, so I decided to sign on for a regular engagement of three years with the colours (an Army regiment) and four years on the reserve (you could be called up in an emergency) because you got double the amount of money each week as compared to someone on National Service. I still very firmly believe that National Service should have continued, two or three years in the armed forces would be exceptionally beneficial to all teenagers today. Why? Because you were taught primarily to stand on your own two feet, to accept discipline, to be fit at all times, and in my case, the fundamentals of leadership. I cannot remember anyone being overweight either.

As a regular soldier I was able to choose which regiment or service I wanted to join so I opted for the Royal Army Pay Corps (RAPC) and thought that, yet again, I had arrived in heaven, because on first attending the Devizes, RAPC training camp I discovered that they provided food, lodgings, clothing, and let me get on with all the sport I wanted. After initial induction training I was selected for a Unit Pay Sergeants course and ended up with three tapes and a posting to the 2nd Battalion The Sherwood Foresters with instructions to sort out all the problems that they had with their pay records and unit accounts.

What a wonderful three years the Army turned out to be, would not have missed it for anything. On arriving at the 2nd Battalion The Sherwood Foresters barracks in Wuppertal, Western Germany, I was given a room which I was to share with 'tiffy' Batten, the REME (Royal Electrical and Mechanical Engineers) sergeant, so on arrival I dumped my kit, thought that I would pop over to the sergeants mess and have a quick drink. Should have checked first.

It was a 'mess' night and everyone else in the crowded bar was in civvies (civilian clothes) save for the poor guy who was the Orderly Sergeant. Most were just back from Korea, the nearest in age to me was 28 and he was considered very young to have three tapes. I walk in and I'm nineteen ! "Are they sending us school kids now?" "It's a mess night, why are you in uniform?" Not an auspicious entrance so I crept over to the bar, all eyes upon me, and just ordered a beer.

They were in the middle of a game called cock fighting. Two people lie on their backs in the middle of the floor with all the others in a circle around them, you lie hip to shoulder and shoulder to hip with your arms resting in a straight line on your opponents shoulder. On a shout of 'go' you lift the leg closest to your opponent into the air, lock legs and endeavour to throw him sideways. I stayed by the bar and after about an hour the champion was proclaimed, one Nick Souch, a very burly ex PT sergeant. He came over to the bar to claim his free drink as the overall winner.

"I'll take you on" I said, somewhat timidly. The bar went silent and Nick Souch said something like "I'll kill you but, OK, if you want to have a go it is your right to challenge me". We lay down, back to back on the floor, I heard comments such as "we'd better go fetch the medics now" and similar. Cock fighting is the best of three throws so initially we squared up by throwing our right legs in the air. Cock fighting is all about timing, not strength. I threw him half way across the mess. He got up said something like "that was a fluke". This time I threw him half way across the mess in the other direction.

He got up , shook my hand very sportingly, said "well done" and immediately bought me a beer. I never looked back, and in fact I never lost a cock fighting contest whilst in the Army. What none of them knew of course was that I had been brought up in the army or at least on the periphery, as we had lived in married quarters with my father whilst he was in the Army, and he used to take me to mess functions where I learnt cock fighting at a very young age.

I did not have to pay for a single drink for the rest of that evening, and what I did not know, was that Nick used to end up winning every cockfighting contest. Now my schooling, or at least the sports side really came into its own as the current PT sergeant got injured, and the Unit was without one for almost a year. By this time I was involved with most of the sports teams, not the soccer I may add as they used to have half of Derby Counties first team squad as NS (National Service) intake ! So I acted as a surrogate PT sergeant for quite a while, as well as sorting out the massive problems that the unit had encountered whilst trying to run their own pay and accounting functions'

However I had a stroke of luck. I used to play in the 1st XV and the CO was a certain Lt. Col. Foster who used to be one center, whilst I was the other. Luckily I had learned my rugger at school, and up and down the Welsh valleys, also the school coach was one, Hylton Cleaver, uncle to Billy Cleaver, the Welsh fly half.

The CO turned to me one day and said "Stanley, how are the boxing team coming on?". I had taken on a number of sporting/coaching roles in the absence of the PT sergeant. "I cannot attend to the team sir", I replied, "I have a pay inspection coming up and Brigade are sending their new paymaster". "Ridiculous" said Col Foster, "see admin and take another clerk off the next draft, this unit's sporting prowess takes precedence over everything". I ended up with the largest but apparently the most efficient pay office in the whole of BAOR (British Army of the Rhine). Also I was not permitted to return to the RAPC (Royal Army Pay Corps) as the Sherwood Foresters wanted to keep me for the sports teams, so they sent one of their own infantry personnel as a replacement for myself, not someone who was a sports participant may I add. He was to be trained in my place, and presumably remained with the pay corps as I remained with the Foresters until I was demobbed. Unless I was the duty sergeant, I was able to go around in a track suit most days. Col Foster wanted us to have every sporting trophy in the whole of Germany!

When I was demobbed I joined Deloittes, who were then the premier firm of accountants, and on my first day I asked where the sports club was, the look of incredulity that I received was nothing compared to the "what on earth are you talking about" response. I honestly thought that the way to get on was through your sporting prowess. I was in for one hell of a rude awakening !

By this time my father had left the Army and taken a pub, The Red Rose Inn on the high Street in Pembroke Dock, so becoming an articled clerk was out of the question due to the cost so I started studying under what were then bye laws to the Institute of Chartered Accountants/Incorporated Accountants. I started off in 'digs' in a small room in Gloucester Road, just behind Baker Street, and after a few days I happened to bump in to one of my very good friends from the Pay Corps, Derek Solt, who had just joined the Pearl Assurance Company in Holborn, so we elected to join forces and share a room as this would halve the living costs.

My last couple of months in the army had left me somewhat more than just the worse for wear, I think it consisted solely of leaving parties, so as the room that Derrick and I had chosen was near the Thames, I went out and bought a folding canoe in order to get fit again. The first day we tried it out on the Thames but it had taken us so long to put together, that we carried it back to our lodgings and wedged it in between two wardrobes. Never did I think that that small folding canoe would, effectively, become part of me and the incidents, as for the one crossing the channel described earlier, would then have me labeled by everyone as a congenital idiot. However our landlady was not amused at canoes in bedrooms, went berserk and threw us out, eventually we ended up in a lovely bed sit, consisting of one large room with two beds and a small kitchen, in Bethune Road in Stoke Newington.

We had a most understanding and exceptionally kind Jewish landlady called Mrs. Liss. What a marvelous few years were to follow in this Jewish enclave in North London as it was at the Bethune Lawn Tennis Club that Mame and I first met, and I do not wish to preempt the third book in this trilogy, a love story, nor the second, all about the great and the good in the business world, otherwise I will be forgetting all about well being and going off at yet another tangent, but as I state later in this book, the path of true love is never that easy. However I was exceptionally fortunate in finding someone who would put up with me, and I might add, especially in the way that Mame and her family did for the next sixty odd years.

Again, when later on Mame and I started our very first business, we were extremely fortunate in finding excellent people who enabled the business to grow and prosper. In the first chapter of this book I referred to the man seeking the route to the top of the mountain, and being wary of the precipices and crevasses that can crop up on the way to the top. Be very, very wary, please do choose a middle path in both your personal, and working life, go too far one way, or too far the other, then you really do have to watch your step. If this does happen then do what Saeed suggested a few chapters back. Stop and Reflect.

CHAPTER 12

Meditation

If every 8 year old in the world is taught meditation, we will eliminate violence from the world within one generation – H H The Dali Lama

I am going to blend the other aids for what I believe is the best way to develop the right attitude of mind, which I believe is essential as an aid to well being, in chapter fifteen but I would like to spend just a little time on a subject very much to the fore today and that is meditation. We should be deeply grateful to a number of most enlightened individuals who uprooted themselves from following conventional careers to explore what was to become a buzz word for a whole host of current meditation techniques here in the West. People such as Dan Goleman, Jack Kornfield, Richie Davidson, Joseph Goldstein to name but a few. They took themselves off to places such as India, Thailand and Sri Lanka, pursued lives with monks, went on retreats, learned all about Eastern meditation methods, and certainly brought a new enlightenment to the greatly over stressed population in Europe and in particular, the USA.

I certainly cannot possibly improve or indeed come anywhere near the excellent resume given by Dan Goleman and Richie Davidson in their book 'The Science of Meditation'. Here they lay out, in very simple terms, the definitions of the various methods which they break down into the deep path, and the wide path, of meditation. The deep path they classify as levels 1 and 2. Level 1 is designated as the really intensive meditation, undertaken as such by those individuals who take themselves off to a cave and just meditate all their life, little or no personal possessions whatsoever. They also include those who become yogis or monks. For level 2, they include people such as themselves who follow deep meditation techniques but have other lifestyles as well.

The wide path is classified as level 3 and above and they detail level 3 as all that proliferation of 'mindfulness' practitioners who simply use the techniques but without any of the deep spirituality that is found in levels 1 and 2. Level 4 they designate as a much watered down version of level 3 such as meditation in 10 minutes while sitting at your desk. Level 5 is level 4 watered down even further. Whatever stage you may wish to explore is great and would, in my opinion, help for whatever the reason was that you were investigating, or simply just exploring, the idea of meditation in the first place.

So now let me give you my experience which again I would not recommend, and is not the correct way to approach meditation; far better to find someone, a recognised teacher who will guide you – without wanting large sums of money by the way, avoid those like the plague. Mine is basically self taught coming from that very young age when I sought to alleviate certain medical problems as those recounted earlier such as relief from Asthma when I was confined to bed if suffering from a severe attack. This was when I simply stared at the bed knobs at the foot of my bed and repeated over and over again 'I will not have Asthma'. That was effectively concentration meditation or *'samahdi'* where you fix your mind on an object and never waver from it. I was also later greatly influenced by the writings of various Buddhist Monks and lay practitioners when I used to visit Sri Lanka, more of which in chapter 21. I was fortunate enough to be introduced to the Buddhist Publication Society of Sri Lanka of which I have been a member now for some fifty years. It was here that I first came across Daniel Goleman as they had published one of his very early articles written whilst he was still at Harvard. Funnily enough in their book, the Science of Meditation, Dan seems to play down this particular article but it lays down the very essence of meditation or at least it does for me.

Although I first used meditation at that very young age as a means of relieving the effects of some nasty medical conditions, I discovered later that you can also harness its powers for stress reduction, relaxation, mental well-being, seeing things as they truly are, the list goes on and on, BUT there is a much greater purpose, and before you start 'deep dive' or serious meditation, you need to have a very firm basis of *'sila'*, which when translated from the Pali becomes 'virtue', but this is a very weak translation in my opinion as *sila* is much, much more. It is the bedrock for all meditation, indeed the foundation stone of life itself.

Basically it is the cultivation of the removal of those traits in yourself that will destroy a person and do cause so much suffering, such as greed, hatred, anger, delusion, and replacing them with compassion for others, kindness, generosity and goodwill.

I cannot possibly cover all the methods of meditation in one short chapter but again, in its simplest form, just relax yourself, concentrate on an object, the one to start with is nearly always recommended as your own breath, and then sit back and enjoy. You can reach such states as altered states of consciousness which some people can also get to by using hallucinogenic drugs, but these have serious side effects, whereas by using deep meditation you can enjoy all the benefits without those debilitating side effects.

You can experience states that far exceed the exceptional heights of lets say mind blowing sex, but herein lies a great danger, do not get hooked on this, this is NOT the object of deep meditation, although a wonderful experience, the objective is another Pali word *'prajna'* or insight. This translation again does not do the word justice, it is defined as reaching a state of being able to see things as they truly are, but I think of it as a state of total acceptance, where nothing will really shake you, you have arrived at contentment to a depth never previously experienced. Some may define it as total happiness.

However do be very careful what you do with this. I used to take weekly sessions at our house in Cornwall with the likes of the very switched on community who ran the Monkey Sanctuary in Looe which was founded by Leonard Williams, a top class musician, a great investigator into the healing power of music and the father of John Williams the classical guitarist.

One week we had a number of ladies sent to us with post natal depression, something of which, probably, I should have been made aware, but wasn't. Some were quite ill with additional complaints, and more than one had been designated as possibly suicidal. I was not aware of this until after the session. I took them down into a deeply meditative state. Not as deep as the state that I describe as really deep because this is the state in which you can experience those altered states of consciousness. As I said earlier, I have been told by users of LSD that what I have described during these states is exactly what you can experience on an 'acid trip' but without all the inherently bad side effects.

My presumption, for which, once again, I have no medical back up as support, is that in each situation, the neurological pathways are temporarily altered so that colours are not just vividly enhanced but the perception is changed, and colours are actually **heard**; difficult to describe and impossible to explain as this really has to be experienced. Music is heard as a colour, but so beautiful as to make you linger in that state forever – and please let me emphasize that herein lies the danger, as the meditation practitioner may forget the purpose for which they are meditating, which should be a much higher goal than simply pure pleasure no matter how ecstatic that pleasure may be.

Having brought the medical group back up to what is normally a very relaxed, happy and blissful state of mind, one lady went somewhat further as she found that she could move limbs that, apparently, had been unusable for a considerable period of time. She wasn't simply ecstatic, she was utterly overjoyed but went a step further declaring that I had healed her when no one else could. Another lady then came up with something similar and although I tried to explain that they had been in a state of deep relaxation, and that I hadn't done any more than relax them, so any improvement to their medical condition was simply down to their own immune system. I kept on insisting that I hadn't cured them, however this was to no avail.

With help from my friends we got everyone off to their homes and all was well, however I have assiduously avoided conducting any such session since! I did not wish to be labeled as someone who performed such deeds when I felt that that was not the case, and that I was not a 'miracle man', a 'God' or a 'Guru'. I told them, very firmly, that it was positive thinking that I had used to help them to cure themselves of any symptoms of their individual illness, but the more I said this, the greater became their demands of me as a healer. It became quite clear to me during these exchanges as to how easy it was for even the most sincere of religious leaders to get carried away by the 'God delusion'. This really was the last time that I have ever lead or conducted a meditation session. Even today I only conduct meditation sessions on my own, for myself, but I do occasionally attend those conducted by my daughter who is a qualified teacher of Heartfulness Meditation and Yoga.

In my opinion I had done no more than relax them thus allowing their own immune system to operate more effectively. However I did have a very interesting conversation with some old friends, Sue and Andy from Cornwall, when I recounted this story to them recently. I had been a guinea pig for Sue when she was first setting up her now very well established aromatherapy practice. When she first treated me I said to her that she had 'healing hands' and that this was similar to the effect on me when I was treated for the first time by Fay, a wonderful physiotherapist who lives on the edge of Bodmin moor whom she also knew, and whose hands had had exactly the same effect on me. In both instances they relieved the pain that I was experiencing, and obtained movement from previously immobile joints.

Sue told me that she came from a long line of Cornish healers and that her grandfather had been a very famous and greatly sought after healer. I then asked her if any of her subsequent clients had made the same observation as myself about her healing hands, and she laughingly said many but they all had one thing in common, which was that they also had this skill or gift to some degree.

When I recounted the incident of the ladies with post natal depression, and their thinking that I had cured them, to my really good friend, Alan, the doctor whom I mentioned previously, he asked me to go through in detail what I had done; I did so and was astonished at some of the questions he asked especially as he asked about my giving them positive suggestions when they were deeply relaxed. He seemed to know far more about what I had done than I did myself! It was no wonder that he was so knowledgeable as he then explained that he had taken an additional qualification in medical hypnotherapy and psychotherapy, long after he had qualified as a GP and anesthetist; his thesis was on the use of hypnotherapy to reduce patients blood pressure.

He used three sets of volunteers from his own practice, the first set being the control group where he did nothing, and at the end of the trial their blood pressures had remained the same as they were at the start of the trial; the second group he used relaxation techniques and their blood pressures reduced dramatically, but then, after a while, they came up again, but it was still below that of the control group, and still much less than before he used the relaxation technique. For the third group he used medical hypnosis and greatly reduced their blood pressure which then remained at that lower level for the remainder of the trial. Whilst the second group reduced the furthest but then came back up again, the third group reduced substantially, and stayed at that reduced level.

He went on to explain that the positive suggestions that I had given the ladies would have most likely contributed to the healing process because they were then able to totally 'let go'. He then lost me in two seconds flat whilst explaining the neurology and physiology relating to positive thoughts causing the release of certain neurotransmitters in the brain. I simply put these various events on paper, I do not wish to, nor am I clever enough to attempt to offer any explanation at all, that is for someone more erudite, more scientific, better qualified, and very definitely someone more clued up than myself!

You will probably see the best results for yourself when you are frantically dashing around and saying "I haven't got time to meditate", take five, take ten minutes, stop, reflect and then meditate. Just try it, you will probably find that you no longer need to rush, that all matters magically fall into place, and at the end of the day, everything has been completed. However may I refer to my previous comments, get a little insight into meditation first, preferably from a really good teacher. I also mentioned earlier that the breath was one of the most popular objects on which to meditate, it was said that the Buddha had forty meditation subjects, and could pick the ideal meditation subject or object for every person that he encountered.

May I, with some humility, suggest another which is most probably covered in one of those forty subjects anyway. Meditate on Karma, the ability to recognise that the actions that you perform have a consequence, perform a good deed and you will receive good fortune, perform a bad deed and watch out. What is a 'good deed' and what is a 'bad deed'? We will all no doubt have differing views according to our own view as to what is OUR version of integrity or morality, and as Polonius said in Act I, scene III, of Hamlet "to thine own self be true", so reflect, meditate on this: never, ever, perform a deed or thought that is not in accordance with your own belief or integrity UNLESS that belief or act would cause harm to others. Or as the Rabbi Hilliel put it "what ever is hurtful to you, do not do unto any other person" I will wait for all the howls of protest to that little Peter 'gem' !!!! - come to think of it, for you purists, it probably comes under *Sila or Metta* anyway.

CHAPTER 12a

Have a nice day

Out beyond the ideas of wrong doing and of right doing, there is a field.
I will meet you there. - Rumi

There is that lovely American expression 'have a nice day', but do you just use it as a form of greeting/leaving or do you think of how you can actually make every day a 'nice day'? Here's my recipe, with no particular order and really no thought, just putting it down as it comes to me. How about starting the day with a big 'thank you', thank God, that is your God or Gods, but if you don't have any Gods and are total Richard Dawkins, then thank your genes, your parents, or your ancestors, just for being alive. Then treat it as if it is your very last day on earth – one day it will be!!

Now can I really try to make your day as it is a long time ago when Alan wanted me to get down in writing as to how my mother and I simply cured illness in ourselves. Then I had no way then of giving that information in the written form. Let me try to set out how we achieve this state in very simple terms, so this is my understanding of what happens:

First and foremost you have to have the right genes, secondly, you have to have the right genes, thirdly..............need I go on, yes, because my belief is that positivity can enhance or even alter your genetic structure. This is simply my view for which I have no medical or scientific back up whatsoever as I am repeatedly stating throughout this book. This presumption is based purely upon my own experience throughout my life. My sister, Penny, possesses this same ability which is standing her in great stead at the moment as she is suffering from the severe effects of chemo following a full mastectomy for breast cancer. She will get over it.

Next comes the tenet that you must have the right attitude of mind, which I think that I have tried to lay out in previous chapters, and which I believe can only be developed upon a very sound base of *sila* which translates *as 'moral virtue'* or the art of removing any harmful traits and replacing these with helpful traits. Very simply, as I said previously, the removal of hatred, anger and delusion to be replaced by compassion, kindness and integrity.

You must treat everything holistically though, you cannot isolate just one 'good' trait such as loving kindness, you need them all. You must also love the trillions of bacteria in your gut as much as you love other members of your family, above all do speak kindly to your immune system, but back that up with right diet, right exercise, right medication, right meditation. Earlier I mentioned that I try to undertake the underlying principles of yoga 24/7, I also do that with meditation and so, rarely, do I need time to sit and meditate, as I am continually meditating or rather trying to, also called mindfulness.

Have a belief system, it doesn't matter a jot whether you put a little cap on your head and go to synagogue, pull out your prayer mat and bow to Mecca five times a day, attend church, go to confession, have communion or just sit in a place of worship in silence. Not have any belief in any God, maybe just simple respect for some of the very enlightened individuals that have wanted to relieve suffering such as the Buddhas, practice yogic transmission or indeed, if that is your bent, have no believe whatsoever, which is the pure Richard Dawkins belief system, and it doesn't matter if your are a full blown Agnostic or Atheist. In other words find a belief system, or none at all, and stick to it, with integrity and love.

Yes, and do eat sensibly, Vegetarian, Vegan or neither, enough pundits and books on that as there is on exercise and well being generally. Your immune system will really thank you, and your ability to control any nasty medical conditions that do occur will be greatly enhanced. Your immune systems ability to heal will be greatly improved if you do keep active. If you cannot make the gym, your bike or the swimming pool, then just walk. Here is the big one, cut out all the excess stress, a little stress within your own personal limits is most necessary BUT do not take on more than you can handle, please. I don't care how you do it, but DO cut out or avoid all those situations that cause you the stress in the first place.

So, can I offer any proof whatsoever of curing or mitigating illness? Yes, here are a few 'happenings'; not medical proof but things that my mother and I have experienced. My mother: crippled with arthritis and only able to walk with the aid of a zimmer frame, but ask her to demonstrate mind over matter and she would discard the zimmer frame, bend over, touch her toes with her legs absolutely straight. You had to see it to believe it. Also curing her incurable cancer related earlier.

Me: the last time I got an asthma attack when I was around twenty and in the army in Germany, and out on one of my training runs in the middle of winter; I was quite some way from barracks, had a severe asthma attack and had to literally crawl back through the snow, but all the time I was doing so, I vowed with a deep, profound intensity, that I would never, ever have another attack of asthma. I have been exceptionally lucky since, in that direction anyway, as everything seems to be OK some seventy years on. I am being 'picky' here, and most cautious in my choice of words, never tempt fate, never, ever, hence this chapter is designated 12A , am I superstitious? Well…………..

Here is another one: I have just been diagnosed with a detached retina, and the eye surgeon to whom I have been referred says he will use laser surgery. Does his nut as he told me not to drive as I mustn't jolt the eye in any way; I simply ignored this and carried on as normal, I had clients to see. He found out, brought the op forward, and when he got me all set for the operation, and in his operating theater, he was furious, "You've already had laser treatment", "no I haven't" I replied, and then it did take me quite a while to convince him that I had not had anything done whatsoever.

In the end he did say that the eye curing itself was not unknown, but quite rare. I did try to explain about my always trying to be kind to my immune system as I just left it to all those microorganisms to which my body is host, and which require me to survive in order that they also survive, the mitochondria, the bacteria, the microbes, in fact the trillions of minute organisms with whom we all coexist and do indeed, depend very much upon each other. As we do with our immediate families, our neighbours, our extended families, and taking it further, to all beings on the planet, and indeed, to the planet itself, Want to go further, research the Microbiome Project, fascinating. Apparently my eye appeared to the surgeon exactly as if the laser surgery had been carried out, thank you immune system.

I have included a few more incidences in chapter 21 but let's get back to those points required for curing or mitigating ills. Very important point now, LUCK. You do have to be lucky, luck does come into it so, I am afraid to mention, is that of having enough money to obtain the right livelihood to pursue the lifestyle that suits you personally. However I was once chatting to a group of homeless people in one of the shady, green areas in Lincolns Inn Fields in London, a district associated with the legal profession and real money, when one of the somewhat bedraggled people swigging meths or something similar told me that he was the lucky one rather than myself, or the people who I was visiting over some very complex legal matters, lawyers, barristers and counsel. "You guys are much worse off than me, you have to worry over your legal matters, enough money to support your lifestyle, the stress of your daily commute, all I have to worry about is where I can get a cardboard box for tonight's sleep". Good point!

Always be up to date with all your medical checks and be very cognisant with all conditions with which you have been diagnosed. If you are not happy with what you have been told, check and check again, get a second opinion if you are still not happy. Watch what you are given by way of 'curative drugs', your doctor may well have been influenced by some medical rep, on commission for a drug company, flogging the pharmaceutical companies mantra of 'we need the profits to fund research so just buy this wonder cure, and prescribe what I am now selling you to all your patients'. Actually, for once, I do have some medical proof, Thalidomide, just to mention one. The whole saga is in my next book but, thank you, just be wary.

So, can I cure illness in myself and others?, not really, what I can do is mitigate the effects of certain conditions both in myself and others. How? - just read this book, but I also do all that I possibly can to prevent illness, which is also of assistance to the NHS and certainly their overstretched budget. I can give one quick solution though, try this, fill your soul with music and your heart with love. That is love for everyone, pure compassion not just for yourself, your family, your relations, your community, your country and for the wider world but also for your plants, if you have them, but if not, for the trees, the woods, the sky and finally, the universe.

Have fun and live for ever, that's what your genes want you to do, or to be a little more precise, until such time as you have reached the limit of your productive age, genes want you to produce further genes, to replicate. That is why they keep such a careful eye on you and go berserk when you overeat, stress, do not look after yourself, but after you are past productive age they tend to relax their watchfulness somewhat, which is why it is much harder to treat many illnesses in your later years.

OK, would you really like a 'quick fix' for all those nasty little 'happenings' that are jiggering up your day, those stresses and traumas that are tending to make your life unlivable. Try a complete change, take an hour off, take a day off, get out in the middle of nowhere. Would you like an example? try the remoter areas of mid Wales, how about around a laid back town like Llanidloes. Would you really like to see a family living their lives with real 'flow'? Google Air BnB for Cefn Cottage in the tiny little hamlet of Twylch in the Dulas valley. If you are stressed

out then I will guarantee that it will work wonders. Can't find it ?
OK, just email me, the address is at the back of the book.

CHAPTER 14

All things bright and beautiful

My religion is to live, and die, without regret - Milarepa

So Mame and I got married, played loads of tennis, had two wonderful children, I would say that anyway, I am, after all, their father, and I do have those somewhat overused rose tinted glasses; worked exceptionally hard, moved from our first home in Wormley in Hertfordshire to Codsall just outside Wolverhampton, as by this time I had moved from being an auditor to an accountant/ company secretary, then to selling copying machines for 3M's (Minnesota Mining and Manufacturing Company Ltd), with Mame and I eventually moving to Bridgnorth in Shropshire, setting up our first business venture for the sale of office equipment (and poaching all 3M's customers and managers, more of which later). This was the start of what was to be a real sixty year roller coaster.

Many of Mame's friends were aghast at her marrying me, but Mame's comment was, quite simply "I could never settle with a nine to five man" and how she put up with me for all of that time I do not know; what I do know is that I would have been a shadow of a person without her unfailing support in all circumstances. Also the support from her mother and father which I did try to repay whenever I could. What was always a huge help to me through what were to be some very turbulent but fascinating times was Mames comment when we first got married "I don't care what happens, I will just be with you, I know that wherever we go, you will always find some way of keeping the food on the table for all of us".

I think that you go through various stages in your life, Shakespeare wrote about the seven ages of man and I believe ended his piece with 'sans eyes, sans teeth, sans everything', I would really like to alter that, I hope that the intense trouble that I was to Mame during those early years was repaid during our latter years together, if not I will just have to resort to that inscription for my headstone 'at least he tried'. I would hope that the final stage of man, or woman, is the best of those seven stages, perhaps a forlorn hope? but that is my aim, which is also another aim of this book. When I was quite young and in the Army, the hope was to die in bed with one arm around a lady and the other around a bottle of booze. Buddhist talk of meditating in the final stages of life, even meditating whilst standing on your head. A bit extreme for me, I would just like to go out knowing that I had completed these three books, that my children and their dependents were happy, and that they were happy for me, and for themselves, to see me go, and to go, if possible, without suffering; in other words a quick exit, out with a bang, here one minute, gone the next, and that the next stage, if there is a next stage, would be just as exciting as those last ninety years or to be a little more ambitious, lets say at least a hundred years as I have still got to finish those last two books!

The business prospered and we moved from Bridgnorth to the beautiful hamlet of Bourton Westwood, just a few miles outside Much Wenlock. After around some fifteen or so years we moved to what was then our holiday home in the rather special, small (and then unknown) Cornish fishing village of Downderry. Originally it was only going to be for a few months, but we actually stayed for 26 years before moving back to our beloved Shropshire, again more later.

CHAPTER 15

Prevention is better than cure

A stitch in time saves nine

According to Cancer Research four in ten cases of cancer in the UK could be prevented. Wow!! How much would that save the NHS. What could I have done then to prevent my Prostate Cancer? Apparently I couldn't, because preventable cases of prostate cancer are unknown as it is not clearly linked to any preventable risk factors. However others are, and I certainly could have prevented those, such as my ever returning sun damaged skin conditions – Actinic Kerratosis, Basal Cell and Squamous Cell Carcinomas – but I need my Vitamin D and I like lying in the sun and the tan used to cover up all those blemishes, scars and veins - any excuse! - OK its risk assessment then, but above all, balance, do not, whatever else you do, go overboard – always try to maintain an even handed, sensible perspective.

Genetics must be the big player here in prevention so we all have to thank our lucky stars for our ancestors, but I am truly certain that in years to come our really talented scientists will come up with the ways and means to defeat most diseases. Life will always throw in that odd ball though and no doubt new diseases will also come to light, it never is that easy is it?

Sleep is a whole book on its own and many have been written, but the simple answer is to have enough sleep for your own needs. If you do not then trouble is heading your way because it is during sleep that your body is able to repair itself.

Exercise – oh Boy! - Just go for it!! - best medicine possible, fresh air and a really good walk will pay dividends hand over fist. However in your younger years do find a sport that really interests you, or any number of sports for that matter, always try a new one if you feel like it, it gives you a renewed interest. Walking, swimming and cycling are generally proposed as being best for overall general health.

Diet, well I just wish that all the experts would agree and more importantly, would not keep continuously changing their minds. Butter is bad for you, butter is good for you is just one example where they swing, first one way, then the other. I suppose that my best diet was during the war, no sugary sweets or cakes, just plain, simple food. However I would think that any nutritionist would look at my diet over the years and conclude that I should be six foot under.

When I was 28 my doctors diagnosed me with gout, due to my love of steak, steak tartar, port, red wine, and told me that if I did not correct my eating habits then my future was pretty bleak. When a little older I went for my annual medical examination which you needed each year as I was a member of the British Racing Drivers Club, and could not race on any circuit without having had this quite rigorous check up first. At the conclusion of the examination the doctor proclaimed "well, you will be able to get into your racing car, but you will never be able to get out of it". "What are you talking about" I replied "you are too fat" he said. Then followed such a dressing down on my love of sugar that from that day onward I have never had a cup of tea or coffee with any sugar in it. Probably saved my life, or at least the prospects of an early grave.

How about the healing power of music. It doesn't matter a jot what your taste in music is, whether it be classic or modern, jazz or hip hop, there are sure to be some pieces that resonate with you, and some that send goose pimples all around your whole body. Try to find those that relax you, those that please you, and those that simply inspire. I believe that when I served on so many patient panels for the NHS, then we were able to create a much kinder, healing atmosphere by allowing people to enjoy their favourite pieces when recovering from illness, as was also proved by allowing pets, dogs, to be brought in to wards. So how about creating play lists, I make full use of a lovely lady who is never rude to me, Alexa, I have two classical and two what I call gentle lists, which is about eight hours in total. My belief is that this does not only aid recovery from illness but is also helpful in preventing illness.

How about breathing?, vitally important, as Saeed is forever reminding all within his sphere of influence, so here is my own little contribution: breathe through your nose, not your mouth, whenever possible. Why, well your nasal passages are your first line of defence against nasty bacteria, helps with nitrous oxide absorption which assists with the metabolising of the oxygen so necessary for life. Also it will keep you calmer.

To assist with calmness, breathe in for four breaths, hold for seven and then exhale for eight; trying to get to sleep, in for five, hold for five, breathe out for five and then hold again for five. You can also try to find which sort of patterns suit you best and you will find then that you will breathe through the nose naturally in time. As I said earlier, I try to live my yoga principles 24/7, my meditation or mindfulness principles 24/7 and all the other principles that I keep pontificating about, but it is helped by starting with the breath. Does it work all the time? Does it hell, ask me what I am like when someone really pisses me off, I regret that I revert to ignoring all those lovely principles, we all do it, I have yet to meet a true saint, we are all human or at least we all try to be human most of the time. At least I hope so.

Let me end this little homily to the prevention of illness by suggesting that you take total responsibility for your own health. Don't just leave it to the doctors, that is if you ever get to see one these days, or the health practitioners, they can only advise and regrettably, then just prescribe, but too often this is just to get you out of the surgery. Too few doctors and with just a ten minute consultation time at that. Try the internet, I used to be about 20% right when I first used to go to the doctors and proclaim what I thought was wrong with me, whereas today, I seem to get it right about 89% of the time. But sometimes I am still totally wrong!! However, in trying to compensate for an increasing population and doctors numbers failing to keep pace, then the advanced nurse practitioners are superb – and usually let you have over your allotted 15 minutes.

Do not, please, blindly accept that diagnosis, check it, recheck it, and if you are unsure, get a second opinion, and a third if you are still unhappy. Diagnosing any condition is not easy, not an exact science, so give those poor, overworked doctors and their assistants a little help; do utilise their exceptional help, advice, kindness and compassion, but in the end, simply accept that you are most probably the person who knows their own body best. Accept responsibility for your own health. Please.

CHAPTER 16

All work and no play (well just a little)

Don't judge me by my successes, judge me by how many
times I fell down and then got up again - Nelson Mandela

Let's move on a few years. I'm sat in my office in Shrewsbury, contemplating how much each of the Office Services companies owes.................in comes Frank Sheridan to discuss his amount "OK I owe you a lot of money" he says "but I've got a good idea, put our two businesses together, you are useless with people, you give too much away, I am good with people, but I'm useless at figures and that is where you are good".

That made a hell of a lot of sense. He was right, I was useless with people because I did give too much away, always did and always have done. So what I have always thought of as the golden years was born without contracts, without fanfare and without any forethought whatsoever other than pure gut instinct - the company called Stanley Sheridan Holdings Ltd. was born.

This later became part of Doloswella Holdings Plc., a public company with a full quote on the London Stock Exchange. Doloswella owned a considerable chunk of Sri Lanka and was engaged in the production of tea and rubber. With just a little guidance from Frank and I it was also to become the UK's third largest provincial casino chain, and thanks to another 3M colleague, Freddie Krebs, the second largest vending operation in the UK.

Frank and I were once addressing a business conference when a comment was made from the floor as to the fact that we were an overnight success. Frank's immediate rejoinder was "yes, it's taken us 20 years to be an overnight success". How did it all start? Frank was from Ireland as was his wife, Shelagh. He started off with ST Garland, the advertising agency and Frank wrote many of the Cadbury jingles which became very well known. He joined 3M's as a salesman later becoming the manager responsible for Ireland.

I was an accountant and company secretary, and had just made a considerable amount of money for my boss, Cyril Austin of H & L Austin Engineering Ltd. So I asked for some of it; Cyril was nonplussed "Stan, you do the books great but you don't make the money, sales bring in the orders, the factory produce them, they make the money." "Wait a minute" I said, "I've just come back with Nick (the sales director, Bill Nicholls) from the Atomic Energy Authority who were livid because I'd slipped through their net, argued for triple the usual contract amount because of on-costs through R & D (research and development), and eventually won the day because of the way in which I was able to interpret (work, wangle, use to H & L Austin's advantage, come on, honesty Peter Stanley!) their contract and terms of reference as drafted by their own legal department - and my costing records".

"I told them you would fire me when I got back because I had not got a good enough deal and the head of their economics board said, somewhat wryly, that you would promote me, reward me and goodness knows what else as he knew what I had done"

"I'll make you a director" said Cyril. Again, very hastily and with no forethought whatsoever I said that I felt that at least a substantial rise was appropriate, so I was leaving and would get a higher paid job or start my own business. I wanted cash, not titles. Cyril fell about laughing, he was not prone to laughing, making money, yes, but not laughter.

"Stan, you'd be impossible in front of a customer and goodness knows what would happen on a factory floor". I resigned immediately, however I was recently married and I needed money to keep food on the table. That's how I came to be with 3M's the rest, as they say, is history. I saw an advert in the paper and applied that evening.

Cyril was absolutely right, I was an accountant and a company secretary, selling was probably my worst choice. However 3M's sales force was legendary, paid their employees more money than anyone else, which was by means of a small salary but large commission, and this was dependent upon how much you sold; 3M's only took on the top salespeople for their Thermofax copying products, and only after rigorous testing and training were they allowed to proceed. Drop out rates were high. I was exceptionally fortunate in that the sales director was the legendary Frank Ford who saw something in me that no one else on the interviewing panel saw.

Nor any of the subsequent sales division who must have despaired of having an accountant to somehow train as a salesman. Few even top sales people made it and my name was top of the firing list for the first three months. Very gradually I managed to bring in more business, they thought that I would fail because my sales manager gave me Shropshire (full of farmers) and Stoke (full of pottery firms). You didn't work from adverts, you created your own leads.

What I did have was an intuitive knowledge of what makes a business tick, and some incredible customers. I was once asked by a potential customer in the Potteries how many machines I sold. I think my reply was "lots" to which he replied "you could have fooled me". So he then showed me what to do to sell the copying machines, as did some other very kind customers such as Joe Bamford whose JCB business was really taking off. I will always be grateful to each of them.

Eventually I sold sufficient to become a member of 3M's elite 100% club (achieving above a pretty impossible target) and it was here that Frank and I first met. 3M's were a marvelous company and as far as I know, still are. I had told Frank Ford at my original interview that after I had learned all I could from 3M's, then I would start my own business. Frank Ford remembered this years afterwards when he invited me to dine with him when I attempted to repay the damage that I had subsequently caused 3M's by nicking their managers and their customers. Frank Ford had kept Xerox at bay for eight years: all other copying machines that were then on the market used chemicals to produce a copy, The Thermofax invention by 3M's was a 'dry' copying machine that used heat sensitive paper instead of chemicals, but it was also very expensive paper at, I think, £9.7/6 and £12.3/9 per ream for quarto and foolscap respectively; please bear in mind that this was over sixty years ago!

I was fortunate enough to find a paper that would work on their Thermofax copying machines, resigned and thought that I could make a better living for Mame and the now growing family by supplying 3M's customers with this paper. An office equipment dealer lent me an office in West Bromwich and Office Services (West Bromwich) Ltd was formed.

3M's were not amused and sent various people to shut me down. When the people that they sent saw my profit margins they were astonished, and then they each wanted to know how, and if, they could benefit; they wanted part of the action for themselves. I set each person up with their own company providing that they bought all their paper through me, and I would just add 5% to the cost price. I also arranged the finance and took a 30% stake in their company leaving them with 70 %. I also supplied the business knowledge on running a company. One of the last people to be sent up to shut me down was Frank Sheridan.

Eventually they all became successful in their own right and bought out my 30% except for Frank as we simply put the two businesses together. Some while after this, when Frank Ford and I were again having dinner in a restaurant in Wimpole Street, close to 3M's head office in London, I made a suggestion as to which direction he should take the copying products division by setting up 3M authorised dealers .

My belief is that this went a considerable way to rectify the damage caused to 3M's by my pinching their top managers (and their customers)! I always had a soft spot for what I still believe is a superb asset to the business community, a company such as 3M's that continually places substantial proportions of their profit at the disposal of their research and development department. Reflective road signs and Scotch Tape came from theses development engineers. A great pity that some of our so called illustrious companies do not do the same today instead of paying their top managers and the venture capitalists - (VC's) . stupidly large annual salaries, bonuses and dividends.

Some of the companies that I had set up eventually became 3M dealers as opposed to competitors. When I lived in Cornwall, long after Frank and I had sold our shares in Doloswella, I was rung by Ian Philpot who ran Office Services (Stanwell) Ltd, we had not spoken for a considerable number of years. Ian's message was "I simply wanted to thank you for setting up my company, it is the anniversary of the founding of Office Services Stanwell Ltd and I just wanted to thank you as we are now by far the largest of all 3M dealers".

We renewed our friendship and I still talk with Betty, Ian's wife, as Ian sadly died a little while ago. His son took over the business which prospered extremely well and is now a market leader in audio visual communications with so many noughts on the balance sheet that even I raise my eyebrows. A short while ago he was able to move into a new £2m house. When Ian and I managed to fund our first houses they cost us around £2k each – I should have kept that 30%!

At Ian's funeral Betty's eulogy contained the following little story: "Ian's territory was Worcestshire, Peters Shropshire. Peter wasn't doing very well so Ian offered to give him a hand. Ian gave a really good demonstration of the Thermofax copying machine to the Managing Director of the Bridgnorth Laundry. He ended his presentation by saying *"and it really is a very good buy"* to which he was cut off in mid sentence by the managing director who stood up and said *"Goodbye then"*. Ian and Peter ended up outside on the pavement laughing their heads off.

The interesting point is that we were paid for what we sold, so Ian had given up valuable selling time to help me, but help for a friend was more important than targets, money or even a job, something that is possibly missing today.

Although office equipment was the original means of earning a living we found that the leasing companies made more money from their finance charges than we did as office equipment dealers so we moved into financing, however we were always short of money ourselves. Having started with nothing we were always reliant on banks. Then commercial finance houses and finally the merchant banks. However my philosophy never changed. I had always found it abhorrent that those doing the work, those at the hard end, received so little as opposed to those at the top.

It seemed that I was doing things in threes. Three years in the Army, three years auditing, three years commercial finance, then three years 3M's − now was the time to go it alone, but I did test matters first with a short spell at E N Mason, they were having a tilt at the copying paper market, so I gained that final piece of experience and set off on my own. You very, very quickly learn the rules of the game. No orders, no food on the table, but first you need a vehicle to get to see potential customers. So I pop in to a rather wonderful bank manager, one Mr Roy Henry Denbigh of the Midland Bank in Bridgnorth, "I need to see customers to get orders which will get money into my account, so could you lend me the money for that please", I walked out with an overdraft of £300.

A short while after Roy Henry complimented me on the car that I drove up in - "You got a very nice car for £300 "he said". "I used the £300 as a deposit" I replied. "It cost a damned sight more than that". "Be in my office tomorrow morning at 9.00am" was the very sharp response. What a superb bank manager he was. For every misdemeanor as regards cash flow, I got sat in his office, read the riot act and then shown what I should do. Even to the extent of sitting next to him when dealing with customers. I owed him so much, not in monetary terms but in being able to learn from his actions as a true bank manager.

His total consideration for his customers was absolute. Always visiting them at their places of work in order to understand their needs. Instilling into them the necessity for honesty and integrity. Years later we were to obtain a banking licence for our own bank, but I have no doubt that this success was due to his very careful grooming during the early years. "Don't lend on the value of the security, lend on the persons ability to repay". The cornerstone of his philosophy - Can he repay, what security and thirdly, what does the bank get out of it! This is not necessarily from the Institute of Bankers text book.

I cannot remember the year of his retirement but it was when they introduced management by objectives, and turned bank managers into salesmen. Not a very sensible idea in my opinion. Roy Henry walked out of the bank for the last time and never set foot in the place again. A brilliant, caring human being hounded out by so called progress.

CHAPTER 17

Oh well , let's give it a go !

Faint Heart ne'er won Fair Lady - Cervantes

I do not think that I ever found it lonely working on my own, there was never time as there were always existing customers to be looked after, new customers, the life blood of any organisation, to be found, checking the paperwork with Mame in the evenings – and she really would keep me on my toes – super efficient as always. My very first customer was Chubb's, the safe people in Wolverhampton, they were invoice No1 and were always extremely helpful. When told by one of my larger competitors that I was just one person working on my own from my house in Bridgnorth and did not have proper business premises, the buyer at Chubb's told the competitor that everyone had to start somewhere , took the business away from them and gave me all their copying supply orders. Never, ever, denigrate a competitor.

Somehow at the end of the first year Mame and I had paid ourselves a large enough salary to eat well and look after our growing family as Roger was now four and Gaye two. We also had a small but reasonable surplus. Time to expand, accounting machine in the spare bedroom and how about some help for me. Enter Michael Clarkson who asked what he had to do, or what training he was to receive. I simply gave him a list of prospective customers, and told him to tell each prospect that he had come to collect the order for copying paper for Mr Stanley.

It worked! He started cracking companies that I had been unable to secure and even many years later continued working as my personal assistant (PA). Some years later he did run into a little trouble though when uttering a swear word in front of a veritable power house of a most religious lady Managing Director, a certain miss Daisy Turner, who was exceptionally strict, God fearing, but a wonderful human being. She really ripped into him, and when he replied that I had used the same swear word that he had just used, she retorted that that was quite acceptable as I had been provoked! In her eyes I could do no wrong but I am afraid that I did not, and could not, always live up to her exceptionally high expectations of me.

She would never accept more than £1000 per annum as salary – long time ago. Her principles and ethics were of the highest degree possible and I was to learn much from her over the years. A most avid Churchgoer, she had the highest of principles and when interviewing new lady workers would always ask "are you a virgin?". If the answer was "no" then the interview was immediately terminated. Wouldn't happen today would it!!. These deeply held convictions that God would always look after you no matter what happened, although not shared by myself I may add, as I always use the maxim that "God helps those that help themselves", certainly enabled her to be an exemplary leader. She certainly also loved her business and once, when the bank manager was going to roast me yet again, she went down to the bank and paid her life savings into the business from her personal account. Again I would ask if this would happen today? Certainly a wonderful lady in all respects.

Shortly after the start of that first year I also needed some help with the servicing of customers copying machines. Could a service engineer be afforded? Enter Frank Jeffs "Frank, I have not got enough work to employ you full time, can you undertake a little in your spare time?" - "No" said Frank "but if I resign then from my current company, E N Mason, then I will have enough to live on for three months and I will come and dig your garden until you have got enough work". "If you are that keen then you had better start next week, I'll simply go out more and get sufficient work" I replied. We never looked back. This is how businesses are born and this is how businesses grow – by teamwork, trust and nothing else but exceptionally hard work.

Frank had a boss, David Ashfield, what a wonderful guy. Very ill at the moment of writing this book but a super person to have as he was able to undertake any job no matter how large or how small. I asked him what he was like at selling but he said that that was something that he had not tried, but would follow my lead. I'll never forget that first day – we had sold absolutely nothing - and it was getting late when we were nearing home, or rather the office, 'home' was something of a misnomer as comfort/furniture took a back seat among all the stock, papers, accounting records and back office typewriters and filing cabinets.

In desperation we popped in to a firm of seed merchants on the bridge over the river Severn on the road into Bridgnorth. We made a very small sale but at least it was something and an excellent training lesson as David said that he reckoned that he could do a much better job than that ! Taught me a lot too, sometimes you can be too confident.

CHAPTER 18

Early Days – late nights!

Nothing in life that's worth anything is easy - Barack Obama

So how do you grow a business when you have no capital, no formal training and someone who is prone to taking risks is at the helm? Answer, you find some wealthy backers, enter Michael Stoddart and Michael Mander. Michael Stoddart was the Managing Director of Singer and Friedlander, merchant bankers with a local office on the Hagley Road in Birmingham, and he, like Frank Ford at 3M's, must have seen something in me that prompted his backing. I had been introduced via the local manger of Lloyd's in the High Street in Bridgnorth, but I had no idea what Merchant Bankers really did and answered all his probing questions at our first interview as if I were in front of a joint stock bank manager (gone out of fashion now but that was a definition of the general type of high street bank that we all know or used to know; they have probably gone all digital and disappeared as well by the time this finally gets published).

Michael was a brilliant Chartered Accountant who had taken Merchant Banking to a new high by setting off from the City and opening branches outside of the traditional square mile, but before investing Singers money he wanted to be absolutely sure that his decision to back me was correct, so he instructed investigating accountants Agar, Bates, Ledsham and King to investigate our rapidly expanding group of companies, originally named Office Services West Bromwich Ltd, but re christened SVO Group of Companies Ltd. I had just messed around with the name 'Office Services' and come up with the initials SVO but Frank Sheridan, when asked what this meant, would reply 'Stanley Versus Others' or 'Sex Very Often'. My lovely secretary Madge Howard (more later) recently told me that she had asked him about the latter definition but never received an answer !

The investigating accountants duly turned up at our head office (our house at 18 Highlands Road, Bridgnorth) and could not believe that they had been sent to investigate a business run from a private house. Upon asking where the accounts department was Mame took them up to our spare bedroom where she had installed her National Cash Accounting Machine, no computers then! That must have really flummoxed them. Anyway they must have given a good report because Michael Mander and Michael Stoddart eventually backed us with their own cash as the amounts we needed to borrow were too small for a merchant bank at that time.

Michael Stoddart had an illuminating career ending up as Chairman of Electra House and is now a big wig at LSE but he made Michael Mander a non executive director of SVO in order that someone could keep an eye on their money that they had invested. What a roller coaster this association turned out to be, but I will always be grateful to them both as no one else would ever have taken such a risk. Eventually I managed to repay both of them and received a lovely gift and letter in return. I have not been in touch nor heard from Michael Stoddart for some time, but was exceptionally fortunate in remaining in contact with Michael Mander who, very kindly, took me for an excellent lunch when I visited him and his partner Derek Collins just before the start of the pandemic. They had a great life style alternating between their flat in Sloane Gardens and their country property in Shropshire, but sadly Michael died a short while ago. I could not attend his funeral because of the pandemic restrictions, Derek has assured me that when it is all over we can give him the send off he deserves, albeit somewhat delayed !

Michael Mander was a member of the family who owned various enterprises including Manders Paints, and The Express and Star, a premier West Midlands newspaper. Their ancestral home was Wightwick, now owned by the National Trust, a most palatial old country house with original wallpaper by William Morris. Beautiful grounds and gardens as well. He was a true gentleman in all senses of the word, most kind. Shropshire seemed to be home to a number of country gentleman and all seemed to be connected. Michael and Derek also knew Barry Jenkinson who was a colleague of mine at 3M's who later set up Midland Microfilm, and his wife , Joy, used to attend painting classes with Michael Stoddarts wife ! Small world indeed!

We were doing rather well with the various businesses so it was possible for us to move from Bridgnorth to Much Wenlock, and to a much larger house in a little hamlet, Bourton Westwood, a mile and a half outside the town with beautiful views right over the Welsh Hills one way, and straight over the top of Birmingham to the Clent hills beyond in the oher direction. As usual the house became my office, and I duly installed a swimming pool in due course, which was put to good use by our neighbours as I literally used to work eighteen hours a day, and sometimes seven days a week. By the way never, ever, do this, it is the most stupid thing anyone can ever undertake. Get a proper work life balance, you're a long time dead.

How do you grow a business from just yourself with no employees to eventually over twenty thousand world wide? I've just covered one way which is to work very, very hard but you also need other people, so, simply employ people who are better than you. That's it. I have some views on this with which no one else ever agrees, so I thought that I would just give an example of this philosophy by extracting one of my LinkedIn discussions for the next chapter.

CHAPTER 19

Leadership , Management – what's it all about ?

Do not follow where the path may lead. Go instead where there is no path and leave a trail – Ralph Waldo Emerson

Ask many purported leaders what are the attributes of leadership and you will quite often receive a macho type response such as guts or courage, but more enlightened leaders may also suggest such qualities as acceptance, which is a wonderful gift as are humility and kindness, qualities which I feel may be somewhat lacking in some who claim to lead in industry and Parliament today. I am inclined to think that these aspects of leadership are more often seen in the armed forces and particularly in the caring professions such as nursing.

The nurses at the world famous Robert Jones and Agnes Hunt Orthopedic hospital in Oswestry used to make signs for their wards, in their own spare time, of the 6 'C's of nursing that I mentioned earlier, Care, Compassion, Competence, Commitment, Communication and Courage. I did suggest at one time that all Directors and senior management had them plastered all over their Board Rooms. They were not amused.

One day I managed to get myself into the middle of an argument over the NHS which also brought in the subject of the fundamental essence of leadership. It all came about when I pushed the wrong button on my computer and got into the midst of a discussion on LinkedIn, and the following is an extract from that exchange. No one has yet agreed with me over my comments, but may I stress that this was a discussion about the essence, *the fundamental essence* of leadership. It was all started by Mike Scowen, a regional director for Llyods Bank Commercial Finance who posed the following question by quoting Dr Maynard Brusman on leadership -

What is the fundamental essence of leadership? Is it the ability to make consistently good judgment calls?

How Emotionally Intelligent Leaders Make Good Decisions – The Human Resources Social Network hr.com

Emotionally Intelligent Business Decisions "Sustainable leaders know that in serving others as opposed to treating employees as servants is the key to better business results, greater team involvement and happier followers." - Dr. Maynard Brusman

Comments by various contributors showing their titles/ jobs/positions as per LinkedIn

PETER STANLEY
Principal at Peter Stanley Consultancy
Great post Mike , thank you very much for highlighting that article by Dr Maynard Brusman. His main point is that we are the servants of those we lead not the other way round. Can we therefore define the pure essence of leadership as personal integrity? putting others first even to your own detriment. For that you need to build on a moral base. Difficult for many of those who reach positions where they are in charge as they are quite often driven by the motivation of winning, of power and of money. This leads to greed and to the fear of losing, as so well illustrated by the events over the past few years.

PETER ALDERSLADE
Executive Interim Manager & Transformation Master with a Practicing Certificate from the Institute of Turnaround

I assume that the contributors to this discussion are engaged in leading change and your posts here reflect your leadership/ambitions. Do you want stakeholders to value you for engaging, inspiring and supporting them to make their decisions, their improvements and their success or for your clever decisions? Which will stand the test of time?

ALEX WOLF
President & active consultant in boutique turnaround, crisis mgtm. and restructuring firm; active USA and abroad
Peter (Peter Stanley) - sorry, I disagree that leaders should be servants of those they lead, except perhaps in a moral sense. A leader must command respect and authority, or he or she cannot lead.

For instance, when a leader gives an order, it is an instruction to be followed, not a suggestion that may be followed or not; and one cannot give orders from a subordinate position. This dictum has nothing to do with fairness or integrity, it concerns a certain necessary hierarchy

Peter Alderslade replied - Alex, I agree with you, leaders are not servants. Neither is leadership to deliver orders to servants. Leadership is to engage with, engender esteem and inspire stakeholders to deliver the organization's vision.

PETER STANLEY
The original post was regarding the ***fundamental essence of leadership,*** the article was how emotionally intelligent leaders make good decisions. Dr Brusman stated that sustainable leaders know that in serving others as opposed to treating employees as servants is the key to better business results.

Daniel Goleman's excellent book 'Emotional Intelligence' brought the discussion regarding emotional intelligence to a much wider audience. However whilst at Harvard and writing on higher states of consciousness he effectively stated that unless you build on a moral base, that is putting others first, caring for others then you will not get anywhere.

Jeff Haden's post yesterday on LinkedIn on leadership reflected this as well .

Becky Reed - Being a leader...is about serving others'.

Lt Col Paul Brunberg - 'Know your people , promote their welfare'.

Steve Shark quoted Roosevelt - 'Nobody cares how much you know until they know how much you care '.

If you are placed in a position of leadership just do it, you will always succeed if you place others first.

PETER ALDERSLADE

Peter S, we may wish otherwise but "unless you build on a moral base, that is putting others first, caring for others then you will not get anywhere" is simply not supported by the facts. Some people do very well by putting themselves first ahead of others. Do you disagree that recently bankers and their shareholders did very well without meeting these standards. What about the serious failings at the Mid Staffordshire NHS Foundation Trust? "appalling suffering of many patients". This was primarily caused by a serious failure on the part of a provider Trust Board. It did not listen sufficiently to its patients and staff or ensure the correction of deficiencies brought to the Trust's attention. Above all, it failed to tackle an insidious negative culture involving a tolerance of poor standards and a disengagement from managerial and leadership responsibilities. This failure was in part the consequence of allowing a focus on reaching national access targets, achieving financial balance and seeking foundation trust status to be at the cost of delivering acceptable standards of care."

PETER STANLEY

Good evening Peter A . Thank you , you have just confirmed the point I was making. The NHS Mid Staffs failure was exactly that - the leadership did not put their people first. If you pop over the border to Shropshire you will see a different picture. Go to the RJAH at Gobowen, every single person from the chairman to the porters, to the odd job man, care with their whole being for their patients and for each other. The nurses in their spare time will make signs for their wards of the 6 'C's of Nursing which they all practice. The same goes on at other locations, local GP surgeries, the staff at the commissioning group. As for the bankers, Private Eye got it right. They listed half a dozen or so of all the top bankers together with that wonderful television personality Terry Wogan and asked you to pick the odd one out, Yes, it was Sir Terry, he was the only one who had passed his banking examinations !!!!The failures were not due to cash flow, lack of planning or incorrect business plans; they were due to greed, ego and fear of losing status and money. If they had pursued a little humility with care and consideration for those who mattered, that is depositors, staff, shareholders, creditors and the general public then they would now be sleeping more easily in their beds. What they needed to do was to practice just a little care for others.

Peter Alderslade

Peter S, despite the Mid Staffs failure and the Banks lack of care their people benefited at the expense of others. They did not build on a moral base, they did not put others first, they did not care for others. They did get somewhere. They benefited at the expense of their customers.

"Unless you build on a moral base, that is putting others first, caring for others then you will not get anywhere" is simply not supported by your facts. People frequently benefit at the expense of others. I do not advocate this, but we would be naive and stupid to ignore it.

Peter Stanley

Peter A, yes, you are obviously correct in that some people do take advantage of situations and do materially enrich themselves. The situations you state are excellent examples. My submission is that these people do not benefit, particularly in the long run. **"For what is a man profited if he should gain the whole**

world yet lose his own soul" This is why I continue to come back to the original post which intrigues me, ' **the essence of leadership** '. This implies the metaphysical meaning of essence i.e. soul. I think that Greg Lustig is correct in differentiating between the essence of leadership and the attributes of leadership. You have asked me for the facts to back up my supposition that good leaders must have a moral base otherwise they will not get anywhere. Servant Leadership is a recognised form of leadership as taught in business schools, do read Robert K Greenleaf , also Lao Tzu, Mark 10:42-45. Daniel Goleman's treatise on higher states of consciousness was, I think, published by the Transpersonal Institute of Palo Alto, California in the early 70's.I think we could exchange posts on this subject for a very long while and we will end up boring everyone to death, how about some lunch to settle this - reply from Peter A – Good idea, lets do that.

There are so many books , theories , pundits and general pontificators , including me, on the subject of leadership that I would apologise for putting this in, but I do believe that it is important which is why I wanted to lay out my thoughts with which, by the way, still no one agrees. I think that they could be right but this is not a manual of how to live your life nor one of how to lead, it is simply the way that I went about seeking a method of managing in a rapidly changing world and again, at the risk of repeating myself, simply say, that it is my hope that it may be of some help to you as the reader.

The main essence or bedrock of leadership, which is totally different to the attributes, schools, methods, textbooks and theories regarding leadership is, for me, simply putting others first, leading by example, accepting total responsibility, allowing those whom you lead to take the credit when things go well and accepting absolute responsibility when they do not. It is not of telling everyone what to do nor of selling them on it– it is just encouraging or motivating everyone by example and just DOING! Simply getting your hands dirty, not referring all awkward matters to committees, not thinking of covering your backside all the time. Dealing with total honesty and utter integrity. However, having shown this chapter on leadership to a very good friend, he then totally shot me down by saying "What about Hitler then", but I think that actually strengthens my argument as regards those misusing their powers. *(Not really − Editor !!)* - OK, so now I do know that none of you quite agree, so I have therefore just added a new chapter - Chapter 22.

CHAPTER 20

Building Empires

Work hard, be kind, and amazing things will happen - Con O'Brien

I was exceptionally fortunate in the people who came to work for me, there always seemed to be a number of people waiting to join our group of companies and those who did so were the most fantastic colleagues for which you could ever wish. They were, to me, additions to my own family and, once employed, they were family. Of course, the members of your immediate family will always tend to bring you down to earth when required – and in my case with extremely good reason!!

Frank Sheridan was a marvelous partner to have and would take all the stress out of a situation with his amazing insight into what makes people tick. Most of all was his ability to be funny in any situation, also an astonishing command when addressing an audience. Not so many years ago, or at least it seems not so many years ago now, I was pontificating to him about personality tests, and how accurate they could be when he told me that he didn't need them as he once had my handwriting analysed, from this, the analysis showed that I had a tremendous problem in marrying the spiritual side of my personality with the money making side. He was absolutely correct, this trait had never been mentioned in any of the Psychological Personality Tests that I had taken, but Frank was indeed, as always, most perceptive, and he certainly was the perfect foil for me in the situations and problems that arose over the years.

On one occasion I was going totally frantic as the banks were threatening God knows what as the money from our backers hadn't appeared. This happened on many occasions I might add, but on this day it was crucial. Frank and I were sharing a large office with two desks in our office in the center of Shrewsbury, when he suddenly said "lets go to the Health Club". "Are you crazy" I retorted" we're in the middle of a huge crisis that could shut us down and you want to visit a health club??

"Yes" said Frank "don't say a word to anyone, we'll just disappear, don't even tell Mame then all the pressure will then be on the banks because no one will have a clue what we are up to or where we are, and the bankers will then have all the worry". We shot off to the health club, relaxed in the Sauna and he was absolutely right, when we got back the banks and the backers had got worried, thought we'd got the money from someone else and so coughed up.

This was the genius touch that he always showed in this sort of situation. On another occasion we were invited to lunch at Rothschild's as they had just bought some of our shares. We had enjoyed quite a few city lunches, but to be invited to dine at Rothschild's was really something. No name outside their offices at New Court and the tapestry behind their reception desk was something else. A gentleman called John Clarke met us and took us to their special dining room but I guess that they had several dining suites of different sizes.

The lunch was spectacular, the wines unbelievable, all Premier Cru, the correct one with each course, the cutlery solid silver. We thought we really had arrived, and after lunch we were ushered in to the huge board room where we were greeted by the managing director, one Clive Richards, and all his assistants. We were both pleasantly mellowed after that lunch and took our seats opposite Clive. Then he pitched in. The fiercest interview that I had ever experienced, and this was presumably to ensure that we did exactly wanted he wanted "We've just bought your shares and you will now ensure that our investment is doubled in very quick time, you will this, you will that......." This went on for half an hour and we never uttered a sound. I just sat there in amazement but Clive wasn't finished yet, he pushed his chair back proclaiming "and whats more the Rothschild bank has been here for one hundred and fifty years" – he never finished,

Frank leaned over and said "so you want to sell it then?"

The assistants faces said it all, but Franks timing always was brilliant, Clive's face broke into a smile, he couldn't help it. We then worked together for a considerable number of years with RIT (Rothschild Investment Trust) feeding us really good acquisitions and we, in turn, taking on some of their quite sticky situations.

We had progressed from selling copying machines to financing the leasing of copying machines. As I said earlier, he leasing companies made more money from the financing than the companies selling them. We then found that the banks made more money from lending money to the finance companies so we moved into banking. We had made our first quarter of a million pounds profit by financing and selling deep freezers, in fact we stole a march on the Electricity Board who had spent millions on an advertising campaign for their units as 'price freezers' so we formed a company and called it Price Freezer Ltd. We didn't have to bother about an advertising budget from then on!

That first quarter of a million pounds became our springboard and we marched onward and upward. We became the countries third largest provincial casino group, the countries second largest vending operation with companies such as Quickmaid Rentals and one of the very largest entertainment groups when we acquired Classic Cinemas. We made a profit of over a million pounds when we sold Quickmaid but we never took any money for ourselves, always ploughed it back into the companies. In writing this I have just realised that you cannot get any dumber than that. Wouldn't happen these days would it !!!! No wonder that my old landlady, Mrs Liss, and all my other Jewish friends in Stoke Newington, used to refer to me as a stupid gentile, in a kindly way though may I add.

There were so many really fine employees but I would be totally out of order if I were not to bring in a certain George Fielding at this stage. What a wonderful guy, we were steaming ahead and

Mame needed to pass over the detailed financial records to a fully qualified finance director as she was concentrating on bringing up our rapidly growing family.

All the most respectable looking candidates had filed into my office and out again but the girls in the office were taking bets on which candidate would be appointed. No one had picked out George, a diminutive figure and previously a skilled forestry worker, but George had wonderful hidden talents that needed to be extracted, prized from him, as talking, especially about himself, was not his forte. Highly qualified, both Chartered Accountant and Cost and Works, he 'did' rather than discuss.

His personal qualities were exceptional and still are today. Absolute honesty and integrity which could never be faulted. When we first started the company we used the auditors as FD's (financial directors) and then tentatively employed qualified accountants, but Mame ran all the day to day accounting functions and I would stick my nose in from time to time as I was also an accountant. You cannot do that when you are a Public Company, so that was when George came into his own. And what a first rate job he did.

Upon attending our very first Board Meeting for Doloswella, in the most splendid of City Board rooms, the Chairman was the Right Honourable Gerald Lascelles, "Fielding" said John Dick, the lead merchant banker "you haven't sent the Honorable Gerald the Agenda". George is the very last person to be cowed by such an attack "You've had the bloody papers Gerald, you know I sent them to you at Fort Belvedre" . "I'm so sorry George" replied the Hon. Gerald, "I must have left them behind". Frank and I had a quiet smile.

Arbuthnot's were a most prestigious Merchant Bank and having been summoned to their beautifully oak paneled boardroom in Queen Street, the heart of the city establishment in London, I was given my instructions; their manners were impeccable, they would have said requested rather than instructed, but I never forgot the words uttered by my original backers, "We have money, you do not, so you will do exactly what we tell you to do". - QED !

At the meeting was the head of the Tea and Rubber department, a very kindly ex Tea Planter, always addressed as Mr. McCloud. "Peter" he said, "we think, that as a newly appointed director and now substantial shareholder via Stanley Sheridan, that you should visit the tea estates". The furthest I got was "Oh" as tickets, times and itinerary had already been booked, however I was totally delighted. A wonderful few weeks visiting a part of the world that I did not know, and a most welcome break into the bargain .

"There is one little piece of work that we want you to do, bring back some money which the subsidiary of Doloswella Holdings PLC, Doloswella Rubber and Tea Estates Ltd, owes to the parent company" said McCloud; I did not foresee the ensuing circumstances!

Flights were not so crowded in those days, and as the flight could be some 17 hours I used to stretch out over 3 seats. If there were many passengers, then you arrived somewhat bleary eyed. Needless to say I arrived, somewhat bleary eyed, and at Colombo International Airport I was met by a huge giant of a man, a certain Reggie Poulier, a senior director at Carson Cumberbatch whom Arbuthnots had appointed as the managing agents for all estates under their wing .

Reggie and I immediately hit it off becoming the firmest of friends quite apart from really close business associates in the years to come. He was a Burgher, which meant that he was Singhalese, but partly descended from the Portuguese when Ceylon belonged to Portugal. He was an ardent conservationist and was recognised as a leading hunter, indeed there is a small island off the southern coast of Ceylon, now Sri Lanka, which is named after his family, Poulier Island .

Reggie was also a brilliant planter and natural leader, Arbuthnot's could not have chosen a better person. Having installed me in the Pegasus Reef Hotel, then owned by Carsons, we departed the next day for the Estate where I was to stay in the superintendents bungalow. The roads were incredible, potholes and bullock carts were much more in evidence than tarmac, however this was shortly after Ceylon had declared independence and they were still finding their feet.

The Marshall's had been managing the estate, Leslie Marshall the workforce and Pamela, his wife, the bungalow, which was most substantial in its own right. It was situated in an idyllic position, the view over the surrounding plantation being exceptionally beautiful with luxurious tropical plants and trees in the garden. The Flame Trees were exceptional beautiful. There was much bowing and scraping when I arrived but Pamela seemed a little nervous.

"I am exceptionally sorry, we have only five servants for you, not six, I am very sorry, very sorry". "Hang on, I said, "servants, what for? I don't need servants"; I was about to have a most rude awakening. What you take for granted in the UK, although nearly sixty years ago, was not present on a tea estate. What was lacking in automated help for general living was made up for by the use of labour, this also applied to running the estates or running the offices. And it was extremely efficient. It was also the provider of many, many jobs for the population.

I always think as to how fortunate I was to have visited the Estates in Sri Lanka, especially being able to meet the countries people, and experience their traditions and values. However it wasn't all work as there was quite a social life as well, and I have tried to give a little glimpse of this in the next chapter...............

CHAPTER 21

Mame's holiday

All work and no play makes Jack a dull boy – it's also a bit stupid for all
of us so let's have a proper work life balance … !!

Mame and I were dining with Reggie, who, as a Director of
Carson's, looked after the tea and rubber estates, but was also
one of the country's foremost hunters within the umbrella of the
Wildlife Society of Ceylon and the head of a well known family.
He lived in a fine old colonial house with his family and a retinue
of ancient retainers; both he and his wife Yvonne were very well
known for their lavish hospitality.

As an agriculturist Reggie had considerable knowledge of the
island's soil and climate, the ingredients of the meal we were
eating came from the farm that he had carved out of the middle
of the jungle. Midway through the meal Reggie asked "How
would you and Mame like to spend a few days on the farm?"
"Reggie, we'd be delighted to accept, when do we go?" "We
could get off tomorrow morning, I will bring my driver round to
your hotel, would 8.00 am be OK?" "Yep, we'll sling a few things
in the grip and really look forward to it."

Reggie used to take me hunting with him; the first trip was
to Yala which was at the southern end of the island. We hunted
with cameras, not guns as we were both members of the Wildlife
Association of Ceylon and in any case, most animals were
categorised as a protected species. To photo leopard you had to
be in position by 4.00 am, elephants would come to your tree
house in the evening. I remembered getting out of the jeep once

to photograph a crocodile beside the river, I moved closer and closer to the croc but he seemed to be asleep.

When I was a couple of feet away, with no movement from the crocodile, a very relaxed voice came from Reggie who was still in the jeep. "I would come back very slowly, he can run a damn sight faster than you." Never taking my eyes off the croc, very gingerly I slid backwards towards the jeep. Reggie always let you know when the animal could move faster than you. Of course, this was always after you were in position, never before!

I only found one animal slower than me – a Python. As a child I had always marvelled at a photo of my father in Australia, he had a Python round his neck. Ever since seeing this I had always wanted a photo of myself with a Python around my neck and one day in Sri Lanka the opportunity arose. There by the roadside was a man with a huge python. A squeal of brakes and in no time at all the python was around my neck. He, or maybe she , weighed a ton. In my haste I had forgotten the camera so I yelled to Mame who found the camera but was not too sure of the settings. More shouted instructions from me but a look of concern appeared on the face of the man who had put the snake around my neck. He was worried in case the reptile was disturbed or frightened as he would then constrict. He need not have worried; I have, or thought I had, an affinity with animals.

I felt no constrictions at all, no tightening around the chest. I was wearing my immaculate white tropical suit. I wanted this photograph like no other. The python did not tighten it's grip but simply relieved itself all over me. Not a very good picture. I could have sworn the python smiled.

Reggie appeared at the hotel the following morning with his driver, dead on time as usual and we were off. One thing you never did was to drive yourself. It wasn't just the bullock carts, the animals, the bicycles or the people; it was the roads. You were never able to drive in a straight line because of the pot holes, so any journey could be tripled both in time and length. The journey went on and on and on. "We must be getting there soon," said Mame, looking forward to that wonderful evening meal with the comfy beds and relaxing time to follow. The jungle became thicker and thicker, more creepers, less light, with the road petering out into a really doubtful, rutted, overgrown, mud track. At last we came to a clearing, bright sunlight again, paddy fields beautifully laid out.

When you first enter a tea or rubber estate the road runs for miles before you hit any buildings so we wondered how far we would have to go before we saw the farmhouse. How large would it be? Would there be the usual carefully tended gardens? The jeep came to an abrupt halt. "Now we are arrived, please welcome to my farm," said Reggie.

"Where is it Reggie?" "You are right underneath it." he said "Underneath it" I queried ?

I looked upward. Above me was a tree house built out of galvanized iron sheets, it reminded me of an Anderson shelter gone nuts. Somewhat bemused we climbed a shaky, home made ladder. One large room, four beds with mosquito nets, one wooden table and the air conditioning was two sides open to the elements so that the wind could blow straight through. Not quite as we had imagined it.

"First we must get the food for dinner," said Reggie. "Can you use a..... .303?" "Yes, but why?" Having been in the army a .303 was second nature but why did we need one "we have to go out to shoot our dinner, there are no shops in the middle of the jungle. We'll bag a few peahen, better than peacock. It will be dark soon, Mame can stay in the jeep with the driver, we'll need someone to shine the headlights on the game."

So much for the eight course dinner. "OK Reggie, how many rifles have we got?" "Just the one but the safety catch is broken. You are the guest of honour so you can have the rifle." I gently slid five rounds in the magazine slipping it in to the pocket of my jacket. At that stage I did not want to load the gun. That would have been tricky, not to say somewhat dangerous without a safety catch.

By now it was getting dark; I was getting quizzical looks from Mame so we jumped in the jeep with Reggie bellowing instructions to his driver. Most Sri Lankans are quite small but not Reggie. He must have stood at least six foot four, probably the same around his girth but a really splendid and imperious figure. "If we can't find any peahen, we'll try for pig," said Reggie. "They are quite easy to shoot, they will charge straight at you so you can get a good shot." Pig is actually wild boar with really wicked tusks that can make quite a mess of you if you miss. One rifle with a dickey safety catch. Some relaxing weekend and Mame was looking even more quizzical.

No peahen, no peacock not even pig. Suddenly a small, dark skinned Sri Lankan jumped out in front of the jeep. Wild gesticulating, quickly spoken with Reggie not bothering to translate. We were then surrounded by something like fifty to sixty villagers. "What's going on Reggie?" queried Mame. "The villagers have had trouble with some elephants trampling their crops and they want us to frighten them away." he explained. "You stay in the jeep with the driver and Peter and I will go with them to see what we can do."

Maintaining the correct relationships with the villagers was essential. They are the life blood of the estates as they tend the fields and look after the crops, be it paddy (rice), tea, rubber or coconut. By now it was dark, off we set, me with the rifle, Reggie with a torch he had fished out of his glove compartment. We were accompanied by all the villagers in a happy little group around us, some ahead, some behind and some just beside us. We could not have gone more than eight hundred yards or so when, all of a sudden, the villagers were not there. They had dropped behind us, then disappeared.

"Where is everyone Reggie, one minute they were in front of us, now they've vanished.". "That is because of the elephants." he said. Quite strange, I thought, especially as they wanted us to frighten them away. By now it was pitch black, two hundred yards on Reggie motioned me to slow down. Something was right up ahead of me. Slowly my eyes got used to dark. When you see an elephant in a Zoo it's quite large. When you confront one in the wild it seems considerably larger. Especially this one, a huge bull with ears flapping and trunk extended.

I tried to ram a round up the breach, it jammed. "Shine the bloody torch Reggie." Out of the dark a muffled voice exclaimed "It does not seem to work, the batteries must have failed." Eventually I managed to get a round up the breach. "If it charges, which part do I aim for, is it that little spot in the centre of the forehead?" desperately trying to remember odd things that I had read in my youth.

"Never mind about that fellow in front of you there is an even bigger bugger right beside you." In these situations your mind works extremely fast. Nowadays its known as 'learning on the job'. "Reggie" I said "if l ever get out of this, I'm going to fire you; what the hell do I do now?"

"Drop your trousers."

"What do you mean, drop your trousers? I'm in the jungle, right in the middle of a herd of wild elephants and you tell me to drop my trousers!"

"They can run a damn sight faster than you, if you drop your trousers they will go for the garment that has your smell on it but if that does not work then run like hell. Go in a zig zag because although they can run faster than you they cannot turn as quickly."

Maybe it was that affinity with animals, maybe it was the fact that elephants are very intelligent and realised that we were actually harmless. Maybe they had never encountered an Englishman before. Whatever the reason they very slowly turned and sauntered off across the river. The whole herd disappeared just like the villagers.

One by one the villagers returned, they were ecstatic, we had driven off the elephants, no longer would they destroy the crops. I was not so sure, elephants, like all wild animals are bent on survival, they do not attack when it is unnecessary. Likewise we would never have taken a shot at them except in an extreme emergency. I reckon they knew that we would not be there all the time and would probably come back later.

We finally made it back to Reggie's tree house laden with fruit from the villagers. This was a marvellous accompaniment to the baked beans which are always the staple diet when nothing has been shot. Sitting around the table, high in the trees with the chatter of monkeys and the croak of frogs, there was one question still puzzling me.

"Reggie, why did the villagers disappear like that?" "That is very simple," he said "it wasn't just that the elephants had ruined their crops, they also killed four of the villagers. The last fellow got drunk and went to sleep on the path used by the elephants. They just trod on him.". "He should have known not to do that." he added.

"Thank you Reggie" said Mame "We will always remember never to sleep where elephants tread!!!

Now I could fill twenty volumes about the various highs and lows of the business world, so could you please render me a really great favour, read the detail in my next book, which I promise to have out by my 95th birthday. Thank you very much indeed, that book will take the lid off some of the myths surrounding the City and The Establishment, especially the way in that we, the populace, are controlled. Also how the Mafia and their leading figures control their empires.

However I do know that my entire earlier life was taken up by the need to bring in sufficient money for all my family, and the way in which I have portrayed this up until now seems so casual, loads of fun and laughter, but it was certainly not like that all of the time, in fact quite the opposite. There is always a balance, you need to tread that middle path, go too far one way or too far the other, and you are heading for disaster. This book will never be finished if I detail the whole of a somewhat crazy way to exist in order to bring in sufficient money to ensure that all your family, and to me, that includes not just immediate family members, but that every single employee has sufficient income for their needs. Note please, needs, NOT wants or desires. So all those detailed business matters, business meetings, and the life of all the various companies in which we were involved, will be in that second book, the third will be that love story, and again, without wishing to hoist too many cliches on you, the path of true love is never smooth. But I can look back on both those episodes, that is the work and the personal side, with exceptional gratitude to everyone concerned, and my most heartfelt apologies for failing to keep a proper chronological order. It makes it more interesting though. *(No it doesn't – editor !)*

OK for once in my life I'll do what I'm told, lets wrap it up for now, how did we progress and what happened to all those business's? We sold out, all went our separate ways. Freddie took over the chairmanship of Doloswella, Frank bought the Old St Andrews Hotel at St Andrews, the home of golf, and later two golf courses in the USA, and I went blue water sailing. This eventually led to Mame and I moving to that great holiday home in Cornwall where I was lucky enough to be able to sail with some of our very best skippers. We originally planned to stay for only a couple of years, but in the end we stayed for twenty six!! The banks, the Gaming Board and indeed even the Gaming Board of Nevada, managed to find me tucked away in a little Cornish fishing village, and I continued to sort out companies, which I still undertake to this day, under the umbrella of The Peter Stanley Consultancy. How many employees, just me; as I said earlier, we had over 20,000 worldwide with Doloswella !! And I will recount which I think is best or at least, the best for myself, and my immediate family, in those next two books,

Another reason for not going on too much about the business or corporate shenanigans is because I am reading a lovely book by Richard Wilson called 'I Cannot be Arsed, or 101 things NOT to do Before you Die' – His last chapter is entitled 'do not write a book'. So, as I do feel that I need to get on with what I consider to be the real purpose of this book, which is NOT about running businesses but to alleviate suffering, I will follow some of his advice, and not be arsed about the business side any longer, but if you arc still curious, then please do email me at pgmjstanley@gmail.com and I will send you some some of my huge pile of press cuttings in order that you can read all about it, if you so choose. If not just ignore them, wait for the next book, which will include all the trials, tribulations, successes, also the failures, and consequences of running large businesses, both materially and spiritually, but please do NOT ignore the warnings re a proper work/life balance. You need to put food on the table for your family, vital, but you cannot do that if you are six foot under. Period. I do not want to spoil my next book by going into exactly what happened, but it certainly wasn't sunshine all the way by any means for any of us. But, as I said earlier, you do have to watch out for those thundering great trucks in the middle of the road, and if you do get hit then just remember that shit does happen.

That next book also details how to get out of those situations as well, but funnily enough one of those thundering great trucks has just come along at the point when I was about to send the finished draft to the publishers. This led me to write this next piece so please do consider the next chapter, dodge those trucks but welcome the kick in the pants that they provide.

CHAPTER 22

'K.I.S.S' - Keep it Simple Stupid

Power tends to Corrupt; Absolute power corrupts Absolutely. - Lord Acton

Ego, greed, power, and sheer stupidity - Wow, that's a lot to tackle in one go - or is it? I've just finished this final draft and ready to send to Bob Fowke, the publisher of this book, who also happens to be a highly respected author in his own right. However I have just had yet another bout of sheer stupidity at the ripe old age of 89, acts which are amply illustrated throughout the whole of this book. Those thundering great trucks catch you out all the time, none of us can wander through life without catching one of these periodic episodes. Here you have a choice, moan about them, blame others, or use them as one of the best learning tools that you will ever be given. Life itself is never simple.

The reason for the title KISS, *Keep it Simple Stupid*, is that it is an acronym which can be a constant reminder for all of us that simplicity is one of the most sensible, but difficult things for a person to undertake, or at least it is for me. Why? Because I am stupid, also because I have an ego the size of a house, and no matter how much I try to tame it, it creeps up like that omnipresent silent stalker that it is. Ryan Holiday wrote two excellent books 'Ego is the Enemy' and 'Stillness is the Key' but the most exacting resume of ego is contained within Sir Anthony Seldon's book, 'Beyond Happiness'.

You will no doubt read many dictates stating that ego has to die before you can progress to a fuller and more satisfying life. I am afraid that this is, for once, just a little too simplistic, it has to be tamed, compromised, used intelligently. I have tried taming it all my life, but then one little thing just happens which will trigger my ego to arise, and that will, generally, set me off on yet another episode of sheer and utter stupidity: so I am now progressing on my final work, which is to tame it. Will I succeed, I'll let you know in that third book *(will you PLEASE shut up about those next two books and finish this one– editor)*.

So what about power, greed and fear? Well you only have to look around the whole world today to see what the lust for power brings to those who seek it. They all have immense egos, but where does it get them in the end? Usually six feet under or in an asylum. They usually accumulate much material wealth, but do you think that people who appear to have every trapping of wealth are actually happy? May I again refer you to Sir Anthony Seldon's book 'Beyond Happiness', he has also written biographies of those right at the top of power, Brown, Cameron and Blair for instance and is thus in a position of knowledge on such matters, and that is quite apart from having been a special advisor to No 10. He does not think that material wealth creates happiness and neither do I.

Humility is a much better trait to seek than power, but again very difficult for those with the large egos. If you do manage to calm the ego, and reach even a small degree of humility then you will be more popular, and what is much more important, genuinely respected by those around you. I have witnessed many people with considerable wealth who live their lives in fear, fear of losing all that wealth with all the trappings that go with it. It is said that those who have everything have nothing, but those who have nothing, actually have everything; often defined as genuine wealth but not in the material sense. However, do let us try to tread that middle path, you need sufficient wealth or income to meet your daily needs, and those of your family, or at least that is my mantra.

So what triggered all this off? Two episodes which, I hope, amply illustrate Saeed's point of the archer missing his target but blaming no one but himself, not the wind, his bow, his luck, just himself. And if you can achieve this, you learn a great deal, especially about yourself; it is similar to learning from failure, which in my belief teaches you much more than success. In both incidents I had done my usual 'tilt at windmills' act by sticking my nose into other peoples lives in order to try to help.

In my opinion both incidents were totally misinterpreted by the intended recipients, but they were, on reflection, exceptionally helpful to me for reasons of my own growth and understanding. Deep anger was expressed at my actions which, on reflection, was probably driven to a large extent by my own ego. My son Rogers' comment, "Dad, you do not have to sort out the worlds problems", Gaye's, "Dad, you are going hyper, do not tell everyone what to do". In both incidents I could have retaliated, but in both incidents I simply followed Saeed's dictate, stopped, reflected and put myself in the other persons shoes.

I think that the possible reason for their deep anger was their own fear, but alongside that was that ever present problem of their own egos. What a recipe for disaster, fear, ego, and sheer stupidity – by everyone !! Who benefited – me, because had my offers of help been accepted then I would have been back to working an 18 hour day, which I did actually try as I was told that I could no longer work the hours that I used to undertake. I managed it, but had I continued to work those hours, then I would have ended up six foot under much sooner than intended. One of these days I will come to realise that my biological age is no longer as it was 70 years ago! It is also exceptionally stupid for anyone else to try to undertake no matter what their age, yes, you can work those hours, but the need for sleep where the body repairs all the daytime damage is crucial, and the stress?? - that always needs watching.

What happened? well in one instance I elected to acquire a company, which, in my opinion, was in urgent need of direction together with a considerable amount of cost cutting. What I forgot was that times have changed, you cannot do in the corporate field today what was done 40 years ago. I think that the management structure feared for their jobs, did not appreciate my comments as to full transparency, and then my informing them what I would do to ensure the company's profitability. Yes, that's stupidity, but the outcome, which was my failure to obtain the company, actually saved me from undertaking a role which would have killed me in the end had it all gone ahead. As I am sure that the excessive work schedules undertaken by both my previous business partners, Frank and Freddie, did for them: at any rate it certainly contributed to shortening their life expectancy. Middle path again, please, do not go over the top in any sphere, an excess of zeal can sometimes be just as dangerous as doing nothing.

Second episode was my failing to consider my age and views compared to those of a younger generation. You always need to put yourself in the other person shoes, consider what might be making that person so distraught or angry. Taught me to be much more careful in everything that I do or say, that's how wars start! Which brings me on to the current world situation – ego, ego, ego!!! What drives what was once a small KGB operative to unleash such suffering on others as Putin has done in the Ukraine. We in the West probably did little to help in the build up to the conflict, but as I am not privy to what goes on in the minds of world leaders then I can only, like the rest of us, speculate. I believe that the absolute power that Putin enjoyed, coupled with his isolation, and surrounding himself with those who were afraid to disagree with him, led to an actual change in his neural pathways so that he could not tolerate anyone's ideas except his own: he became so engrossed with his own concept of reality that he made the most terrible judgment.

However please let me tell you of one of my experiences of Russia pre Perestrokia; some time in the 1960's Mame and I, together with Frank and his wife Shelagh, motored around the Autobahn on our way to a trade show in Leipzig, then part of Eastern Germany. Every time that we were stopped by the East German Police, who immediately cocked their guns in a most threatening manner, we got used to simply putting our hands in the air, bending over the bonnet of the car and reciting all our personal details. The fear that permeated the whole area was horrific. On arrival back in the Western sector, having come through Check Point Charlie and 'the corridor', we marched in to the first hotel that we saw, straight up to the desk, stood rigidly to attention and immediately, once again, started reciting our personal details, passport number and so on before being stopped by the kindly west German hotel operative who said "relax, please, just relax, you are in the West now". They saw this reaction from those leaving the East German sector all the time. We had been there for less than a week!! To a degree our neural pathways had changed, even in that small space of time. Which is what I believe happens to anyone subjected to brow beating, so what hope is there for someone who has a position of absolute power and surrounds himself with only those who will praise him? Conversely, this speaks much of those who have had to live under a totalitarian regime for years, and yet still retain their integrity, as millions of silenced, ordinary Russian people do today; however I am certain that their spirituality will help them greatly. This is something of which I continually remind myself. It is also something upon which, in my personal belief, that we should all reflect.

That changing of the neural pathways is covered in much greater detail in my next book, but just ponder the effect of being jettisoned into a position of power, and how you would feel if everyone was kowtowing to you; you do not have just a blown up idea of your own importance, but an utterly distorted view of all situations, a total lack of all reality. Consider also the other end of matters, what happens if you are confined to a Gulag or to a Prison, with no idea of any release date? Read or better still talk, if you are acquainted with any, to survivors of the Japanese prisoner of war camps. Read 'The Railway Man' by Eric Lomax. It took him a lifetime to utter just one word as to what happened to him whilst a prisoner of the Japanese. I have found this same trait with all Far East POW's that I have known, including a close associate who had been banged up in Changai during the war. He never mentioned it once.

I suppose that this is why I favour my views on leadership, as for me, one ounce of compassion is worth ten million tons of the trappings of power and all that it brings.

CHAPTER 23

Unexplained happenings

There are more things in Heaven and Earth, Horatio, than are dreamt of in your philosophy - William Shakespeare

Another quixotic title for a chapter? Possibly, but it may be a good time to pop back to the belief systems, simply to let you know of a few experiences for which I have no explanation, and for which I have indeed, never sought. For a long time I had this section as separate to the main book; I thought that were I to put some of these events on paper, then most people would have labeled me a total basket case.

However having read ' The Art of Dying ' by Dr Peter Fenwick and his wife, Elizabeth Fenwick, I was totally astonished as many of the situations that they describe have been 'mirrored' by myself in one way or another. Dr Fenwick is a highly respected neuro-psychiatrist and a Fellow of the Royal College of Psychiatrists. We talk too little about the process of dying and I do highly recommend their book .

Belief systems can have many forms and can manifest themselves for good or otherwise, the good we know about, but what about the effects of, say, voodoo upon someone who truly believes in black magic? Many, many documented cases of people dying of no medical cause save for the fact that they had been told by a voodoo practitioner that they were going to die.

Some time ago I rang Beatte, the daughter of a very good friend, John Richardson, to find out how he was, and she replied "how did you know" to which I said "know what ?". Beatte then replied "that he died a couple of hours ago," - "I am very sorry to hear that" I said, "we always used to ring each other at almost the same moment even if we hadn't spoken for ages". The last time that I had rung Beatte or John must have been a good six months previously. Yes, I know what you are going to say, coincidence.

It must have been well over forty years ago now when Mame was visiting her aging and somewhat ill parents in Plymouth, leaving me in the house in Shropshire with full instructions on how to look after, feed, care for, and generally cosset, her utterly beloved family cat, Jumbo. He was an absolute one off, highly intelligent, mischievous , charismatic and somewhat special as he had six claws on each paw (he used to literally run up the patterned wallpaper when a kitten).

One night he failed to appear for his supper, odd. Didn't see him at all the next day so I set out looking for him everywhere, but there was no sign, no trace. Bourton Westwood House was positioned in between a couple of farms, with one or two smaller cottages nearby. Jumbo was not to be seen. I then rang all the neighbours and near neighbours, eventually getting a call from John who used to farm the lower farm, his father and brother David used to farm above us.

"I think there might be a cat in the hedge in the lane near us" was the message. Quite late at night I shot out to have a look and eventually found Jumbo in the hedge near Johns farm. He must have jumped out of the hedge after some wildlife, was hit by a vehicle and must have died instantly.

I cannot describe the feeling of mortification, of sorrow, of regret, and of utter remorse. How could it have happened, how could I have let it happen, I was totally horrified, gathered him up in my arms, and carried him back up the lane towards our house. He was a real member of the family, beloved by all of us, and each step that I took seemed to make everything worse.

How could I tell Mame, how could I live with the knowledge that I had allowed this to happen. I really was beside myself, went in through the gates, got him into the garage, and then something happened for which I have no explanation whatsoever. I laid him, very gently, on a blanket in a cardboard box, when all of a sudden I had an enormous felling of warmth, love, well being, and of bliss that cannot be described. With it a sense, that is the only way in which I can describe it, of a knowledge that he was exceptionally happy, that I was not to worry in any way at all, and it was not my fault. With a happening like that I would normally have beaten myself up and never forgiven myself even forty years later. Even to this day, I always feel happy, because I have the knowledge that, somehow, he is infinitely happier.

Shortly after Jumbos death we moved to that holiday home of ours, named Bali Hai, in Downderry, in Cornwall; it was to have been for a couple of years, but we did stay a lot longer. When we moved in to Bali Hai, the house to our left had not been finished but was being built by John for his wife Jean and their son, also called John. John senior really used to beat himself up, so I tried to help, and one day lent him some of my self hypnosis and relaxation tapes. He asked when I wanted them back, but I said that he should keep them as I was having to go to Bristol for a few days. I think that we were only away for three days, but during that time he had gone up the Hessenford valley, which was on the way from Downderry to Plymouth, welded some piping to his exhaust, locked the car, turned on the ignition and killed himself.

I also found that he had taken the trouble to return my tapes, neatly packaged, not long before he had committed that fateful act. Just before his funeral Jean invited us to their now finished house next door. When we went in to their lounge all Johns relatives were sitting down the left hand side of the room, and Jean's to the right. No one was speaking, just glowering, and the atmosphere was horrific.

I looked from side to side with a smile on my face. Total silence but more glowering. "wasn't that a brave and brilliant thing that John did" I said "not many people have that sort of courage". I thought Mame was going to kill me, her looks certainly said it anyway. All of a sudden everyone started talking, relaxing and both sides of the family were now visibly reacting with each other. Mame was still going to kill me until Jean came up and thanked me profusely for, as she said, defusing a somewhat awkward situation.

I never gave it another thought until John's funeral. We were all sitting in the Church, chatting away happily to whoever was next to us, and then John's coffin was brought in. Again it would be difficult to put into writing the feeling that simply engulfed me as the coffin passed, sheer bliss is insufficient, simply a feeling of "thanks" - "great" - everything is fine, everyone just be happy". An all enveloping feeling of sheer love; with it a feeling or sensation that again is impossible to describe.

One of the reasons why I feel that a real cause of depression is down to genetics is the way that Jean's son, John, reacted after his fathers suicide. His condition deteriorated over the next few years. On one occasion Jean came running in to our house in a very frantic manner "please help, John has an axe and is going wild with it" I saw John in the garden whirling the axe around so I simply popped out and said "hey John, can you chop us some wood at the same time please" and he then seemed to return to normal in a very short space of time.

This did not last as his condition deteriorated further and further over the years, refusing to eat, staying in bed for days at a time, never leaving the house. He emulated his father in that he too committed suicide almost ten years to the day that his father also took his own life. They were both lovely people and a delight to be with on all occasions.

I am still loath to actually include any of this, and these are only a couple of instances, there are many, many more. I would have kept it all on the back burner had I not read 'The Art of Dying'. Were you to postulate this to a neurosurgeon then the most likely explanation is that my brain releases various chemicals that produce a feeling of euphoria - dopamine, serotonin, oxytocin, endorphins **- *and yet – and yet ????* -**

Dr Peter Fenwick, as the eminent neuru-physchiatristt that he is, has investigated such happenings and relates only some of his experiences in his book. His research is most enlightening. So are others who are again far more qualified than myself to expound on such matters: I rang to speak to my oncologist the other day, but as he was engaged I spoke instead to the matron at the cancer center where he practices. Here was someone who did not know me, save for my case notes , so I really did think that I would get a total rebuttal, or at the very least some skepticism to all my 'no explanation' stories.

Far from it, "You would be quite astonished, the general public are not aware of the considerable number of times that we can find no medical reason for the cancer going into remission or simply vanishing" she said, "and it is far from being just isolated cases". However let me please add a cautionary note here, none of us can utilise our minds to the extent that we always succeed in healing either ourselves or other people. I know of no one who has put off dying, that happens. Period. Should a disease be so far advanced that the body is ravaged, such as cancer that has metastasized, that is spread from the primary cancer to multiple locations within the host body, then you have a real problem. I do not know the cause of cancer nor do I know of any overall cure. Research, for which funding is always most gratefully appreciated by the cancer research charities, is ongoing.

This is also pertinent to so many other diseases for which there is no known cure. All that I have ever done, and that from a very early age, is to attempt to relieve the suffering. Nothing more. It is probably due to this that I continually seek to alleviate or better still, prevent, nasty conditions rearing their wretched heads within myself.

On a personal level I would always plump for a good death at whatever age. So what is a good death? as far as I am personally concerned it is a quick one, without suffering. Many people say that dying, if it is instantaneous, is easy, living a life of service to others, without considering rewards, is far, far more difficult. Major beliefs always recommend taming your own ego well before death. Buddhist belief is most stringent on this point, Christianity (the parable of the grain of wheat) less emphatic but still a main driver.

I haven't got to first base on this one so will probably, as far as my friends in the far east are concerned, come back as an animal of some sort, so when they gently chide me on this point, I always plumb for coming back as a Dolphin or an Elephant, but if I am feeling very antagonistic, belligerent or annoying, then I say as the king of the jungle, a Lion or if not a Great White, which is not afraid of anything.

Having dived with all forms of marine life, I found that sharks are actually quite shy, unless food is around, Barracuda will circle above you, indicating that you are in their territory, so leave, immediately, huge Jacks, at quite low depths, used to simply sidle up to you and bump or nudge you. Some are just inquisitive, some just happy to swim with you for what appears to be company, however no matter how much I would talk about empathy with animals or marine life, I really do not fancy putting this to the test with a Great White, nor for that matter with a Lion !

CHAPTER 24

So what about the really
way out happenings -

Unexplained events can set you back or set you up.
It's all a matter of perspective - Mary Anne Radmacher

So why has it taken me so long to put all this down on paper? - or rather tap in in to a computer? Probably because I thought that the previous chapter and especially this one, together with some of my final conclusions, were far too way out to be voiced: I'm going to put them down anyway. They are what happened to me for which there is no back up, no research, no verification, just my memory, no comments on that please !!! There is also another book that I have been fortunate enough to find at my local library, 'After' by Doctor Bruce Greyson. Again dealing with death, near death, and his research stretches over something like forty to fifty years; a most respected psychiatrist, however I found that, once again, as with Peter Fenwick's book mentioned in the previous chapter 'The Art of Dying', there were so many instances of a similar, related or mirrored happening.

There is another reason, and this time from the literary world; when I first started writing this book/novel/memoir/self-help/ meanderings or simply a treatise on well being. my super efficient secretary, Madge Howard, from what seems like five million years ago *(hyperbole!! - yes miss editor – I know)*, actually 45 years ago, told me to always write in the way that I had started formulating the narrative in this book, and never allow anyone from the technical side of writing to alter my style in any way whatsoever. No if's, no buts, the writing community will hate it, but not the reader for whom this book is intended – and obviously that is you if you have managed to get this far!!! I do hope that she is correct. Madge is a far better writer than myself, as was her husband Joe, who joined me from a highly reputable city institution who were trying to screw me very early on in my career. All of which is detailed in my next book.*(do shut up your next books and finish this one - editor)*

Once again, let's start at the beginning which is always an excellent place at which to start!! No matter how many years I seem able to carry on I have never, in my inward self or inner self, ever altered. It was Ruth's mothers 90th birthday a few years ago, I had great fun with the four/six year old's, kicking balloons all over the place. I was more at home with them than talking to all the other guests, and I was 87 at the time. My outer self has created chaos, saved lives, loved and been loved. My inner self has never altered, I am most relaxed when in extreme danger, I just leave everything to that inner self. Crazy, yes but I am simply putting this down as it is, not how it is supposed to be.

Gaye once gave me a book called The Spiritual Wisdom of India by Lisbeth Ejlertsen, in which Lisbeth described an incident where she tripped, found herself falling, but then time, literally, stood still, suspended, an incident that she described in some detail. I am sure that this does happen to many of us at certain moments, especially stress or danger, and I am certainly not the first person to highlight this sensation. Many have commented on the way that time 'fly's by' when we are concentrating, and an hour can go by as if it were just five minutes, driving up motorways for instance. Again, may I repeat that many of these instances are simply what happened to me, I have no explanation for them whatsoever, but certainly Bruce Greyson, in his book that I mentioned at the start of this chapter, at least has a go at a scientific explanation. He is only a few years younger than me, but a most respected doctor, psychiatrist and award winning author, so may I say again that his book is called 'After' and he has investigated the separation of the mind, consciousness and the brain in some detail.

I must have been very young when I first realised that there was an 'inner' side, a subconscious element to existence, and would certainly not have been able to put the sensations in to words at that age. Indeed I am not able to do so today, any more than trying to elucidate the manner in which my mother, or myself, could describe the way that we used to 'cure' ourselves of different ailments. These different 'happenings' have continued to crop up; I do not know my exact age when I discovered that I could 'programme' my dreams; which was hilarious as I taught myself, in my dreams, to 'fly' way above the ground, above the trees, and to soar way up in to the sky, but if I ever thought, in a dream' "wait a minute, you can't do that, you're dreaming, you are in a dream" then I would start falling back down to earth again. I would simply think, just before going to sleep, very deeply of wanting to be able to fly in a dream and then, perhaps not that same night, but maybe the next one, just fall asleep and when starting to dream just stretch out my arms and take off! Actually a very uplifting (unintentional pun) sensation! Another little quirk that I was able to achieve at a very young age was to 'split' dream, that is have one side of my mind in the dream and therefore asleep, but the other in the bedroom where the other half of me, that is the other half of my brain, my mind, was awake.

Another time I attended a meeting which was being addressed by a most spiritual lady who talked of deep meditation and the power of the mind. Just for a laugh I thought that I would concentrate my mind on hers to see if my mind was stronger than hers, I did not expect any reaction whatsoever so concentrated hard on her forehead, and received what can only be described as a huge kick in the teeth, except of course it was my head. It was like being struck by a thunderbolt, so much so, that I was jerked back in my chair, totally stunned. She went on, smiling sweetly, and was not in the least put out. I never tried doing that again! Again it could, of course, have simply been a coincidence of some sort.

There have been many other instances, some of which involved Mame, which I am leaving until book three, but let me end this chapter by telling you of a little incident whilst traveling from Downderry to Bristol. I had just left Plymouth and was motoring north on the A38 which was in the course of having crash barriers erected in order to separate the carriageways. Only a few stretches had been completed in order to make it a safe dual carriageway. The traffic was quite heavy in both directions, dark with the usual headlight glare.

Suddenly, in what seemed extreme slow motion, a car started to glide slowly from the opposite dual carriageway right across the central reservation, and right into my path of travel. I desperately attempted avoidance procedures, but it clipped my rear offside sending me spinning across our lanes and across the central reservation straight into the oncoming traffic on the opposite side of the road. I knew that my number was up and thought "hey, for once this chaos is not caused by me. I've got all the share certificates in the boot, I cannot kick the bucket now, I've got to get to that meeting tomorrow". I was spinning around with all the headlights of the lorries and cars about to hit me when it all went quiet, a depth of silence which again, cannot be described, and it seemed to last forever. There was a horrendous bang and I found myself wedged up against the crash barrier on the opposite side of the road to that in which I was traveling and facing back towards Plymouth, in other words the direction from which I had just come.

The car was a total wreck, but I managed to climb out through the roof. On the opposite side of the dual carriage way there were umpteen cars in quite a pile up with shouting and screaming, but apart from that the silence, and the depth of darkness, it was really eerie. I dashed over the road to see what I could do, and the driver of the car that had drifted across into the path of all the oncoming traffic was a total gibbering wreck, so I did what I could to calm him down, and some of the other people as well. It turned out that he had fallen asleep at the wheel!

Yes, I did manage to get a lift to Bristol and was able to get those share certificates out of my wreck of a car and did, the next day, complete the deal. However I cannot explain how I got out of all that, the car was a total write off! And I cannot explain the quiet, the depth of the silence and the utter, utter blackness, nor the slowing down of time.

As I said previously, I have simply put down on paper what happened to me and would not have the temerity nor the knowledge to ever attempt any explanation. Dr. Peter Fenwick details his lengthy research into patients at the point of, or near to the point of death, whilst Dr Bruce Greyson details considerable research, again over forty years or more into 'Near Death Experiences', that is people who should not have lived or people who had been pronounced dead, and were then resuscitated. In other words people who had just passed the point of death. All cases bear remarkable similarities and cannot simply be dismissed as 'one offs'. Science has proven facts which are taken as absolute truth until some other research throws up evidence of some other facet, which then becomes the new 'fact' or 'truth'. For instance the earth was thought flat until it was proved to be a sphere. I have simply set down what happened to me, nothing more. And I have many, many more similar instances.

CHAPTER 25

Downderry to Baschurch

There is no time for cut-and-dried monotony. There is time for work.
And time for love. This leaves no other time. - Coco Chanel

The money from the sale of the shares in Doloswella Plc has long gone, but Mame and I are making a comfortable living from my consultancy practice, Peter Stanley Consultancy. Mame is doing most commendable work, first as a Samaritan volunteer, and then as a local director for them in the South West. She is also serving meals on wheels, potato lunches for the village, and fund raising for various charities, one of which was the local community bus for which they all received the Queens award. Their efficiency and organisation put most of my business clients to shame. I too, offered to help, however, for some reason, they would never allow me to drive the bus !!

Once I went to buy a Zoo in Bognor, the owner was one, Jack Bethell, it turned out that he was an ex BOAC pilot turned sail maker, Arun Sails, what he wanted to do was sell the zoo and have sufficient time to test his revolutionary sail designs, which were based on his aeronautical skills. Same principal, the wind pattern over the wings of an areoplane is very similar to the wind pattern over the sails in a sailing boat. "I want to test some cruising chutes" he said "great idea" I responded. The result was that he and his son Jeremy, a great sailor, together with George Fielding, who also loved his sailing, and myself set off into the wilder stretches of the Atlantic. The objective was to test these cruising chutes (slightly smaller than spinnakers and easier to handle). They are the somewhat larger sails than those that you throw up (hoist) at the bow of a sailing boat if you are sailing downwind; spinnakers are normally used when racing, but the slightly smaller cruising chute is probably more suitable when cruising.

Eventually we were away some six or seven weeks, sailed down to the Azores with gales all the way and dead on the nose, in other words, sailing directly into the wind. The wind speed never got below a force 7, that is near gale force, but the wind was constantly blowing a 9 (gale) or 10 (storm) and above. I came off watch once, absolutely shattered and had just got into my bunk, immediately fell asleep when there was an almighty crash, and everything in the cabin came crashing over me, the door burst open with George proclaiming "we've been knocked flat, taking some water, better get life jackets". "I'm too bloody tired" I exclaimed and promptly went back to sleep, soaking wet among all the debris. When you get knocked flat it is because a huge gust of wind has caught the side of the boat and knocked it down flat on it's side in the water, we were very lucky as it righted itself without the loss of the mainsail, but we did lose a few other pieces of equipment; luckily not the fresh water which was stored in plastic containers and rigidly tied to the superstructure. We were exceptionally fortunate as we were right off the main shipping lanes and out of radio contact. It was the year when all the single handers were getting flattened and rescued. This is a race for sailing yachts with only one occupant (thus 'single handers'), who race from the UK to the Azores. There were four of us, but we weren't racing, however we found it strenuous enough just on 'Navy Watches', that is each of us would be on watch during the twenty four hours alternating between five, four hour watches, with two watches of two hours each. The latter being known as the 'dog watches'. Single handers have to, effectively, be on continuous watch, but they do manage to 'cat nap'.

We actually helped one of the single handers after he had finally got his boat up-righted and was eventually towed to the Azores. A whale had flipped it's tail fin right in front of his boat causing a mass of water to flood him and a lot more besides. A lovely guy who, when we got to the Azores, used to phone Mame to pass messages to his girl friend; he could not get through himself. He eventually got fed up with normal life and decided to try to sail round the world twice without stopping. We waved him goodbye when we set off back to the UK from the Azores, he went one way, we went the other.

I suppose that this was yet another time when I should be exceptionally grateful to that Guardian Angel, as during this time I was able to sail with a number of our leading skippers; there were many advantages to living in the South West! One of those skippers was a brilliant yachtsman, Aubrey Long, who, having trusted me with the helm, went absolutely berserk when I ran over a pallet that some idiot had left floating in the middle of the Ocean. It damaged all his precious (and very expensive) racing gear attached to the keel. When ashore I then then spent many hours scrubbing the bottom as a punishment.

When we first bought the property in Downderry, Roger had rescued a wonderful Border Collie, who, as the runt of a litter at one of the local farms, would not have had a very long or pleasant existence. Roger named him 'Bumper', and Roger, having just finished University, looked after the house in Downderry when we first purchased it. He eventually went to London to work for Coopers and Lybrand, which became PricewaterhouseCoopers. He took Bumper with him to London, but left us with his skis, his cat and his girl friend!

Eventually life was impossible for Roger to have Bumper whilst studying to be an accountant in London, so Bumper ended up with Mame and I back in Downderry. Wonderfully intelligent, he really did become one of the family, getting into all sorts of scrapes, but somehow or other always getting out of them. We both totally treasured the time that he was with us.

I carried on with the consultancy practice but Mame thought that I ought to take it easier and persuaded me to apply to become a watch keeper with the newly formed National Coastwatch Institution (NCI). She thought that that would stop me working, fat chance! I rang the station commander, a certain

Wing Commander Ian Chivers, who had previously directed the Hercules search and rescue planes from Plymouth; having been grilled on my experience he said "you'd better come up and do some watches then".

I went up to the watch station, put my name on the list that I saw on the wall, and started doing my watches; I think that they were then of four hours duration and just one person. The NCI had only recently been formed in Cornwall in 1994, officially it was because of the danger to which Cornish fishermen were exposed, but I think that it was, effectively, the MCA (Maritime and Coastguard Agency) who decided not to continue with visual watches but to rely on computers. Daft, sorry, but in my opinion you need to keep a visual watch at all times. Try being on the helm of a small yacht at night crossing the Bay of Biscay, and then observe those huge ocean going tankers navigating without, in my opinion, a proper visual watch. You need eyes in the back of your head!!

Once again, what a fascinating time I had within the NCI organisation, I was on my second or third watch when the door burst open and a somewhat rotund, but fierce beyond belief lady, hurtled inwards "Who are you and what the hell are you doing" she exclaimed "Peter Stanley" I replied, "and I'm on watch keeping duties", "I wondered who on earth this Peter Stanley was who appeared on my lists, who told you could keep watch, which training course have you been on?" What followed then was hilarious, this was the lady whose nickname was 'The Rottweiler'. She kept everything in first class order on the station; a brilliant organiser with a fearsome reputation, but what a superb job she did. On this occasion it appeared that the station commander, who obviously disliked rules just as much as I did, forgot to tell her that he had told me to go on watch.

Afterwards I did complete my watch keepers course under the surveillance of Ian Chivers, and the other senior watch keepers who, like Ian, had exceptional experience in Maritime matters. On one occasion I was slightly out on my perceived bearings and in answering the instructor, I quite innocently replied, "It doesn't matter, it was near enough". "No it wasn't" thundered the instructor who, before he retired, had commanded the worlds largest ocean going tanker "when I'm going through the Panama Canal I've only got inches to spare, Port or Starboard, do it again and this time I want 100% accuracy". Eventually I also took a senior watch keepers exam as well, sorted out a number of pressing admin and accountancy matters when not on watch, became a trustee, only four meetings a year said the NCI chairman, I was back to eighteen hours a day seven days a week on occasions – and all voluntary - so much for Mames idea of getting me to slow down! But it was all worth it, I was able to get a millennium grant for new equipment, attend the most meritorious of meetings, and eventually ended up auditing the Rame Head Stations accounts after I had retired as a trustee. I cannot put into words the rewards that you receive from undertaking such voluntary work. It was just as Mame had found from her work with the Samaritans.

CHAPTER 26

Baschurch to Boughton

One must work and dare if one really wants to live - Vincent van Gogh

Roger rings from Moscow where he is PWC'c lead partner for Fraud and Forensic in central Europe. "Dad, we've bought a farm and my partners have given me a years leave of absence to sort it out", "OK" I say "where is it?" "Whitchurch", he replies "actually it is near the little hamlet of Alkington, right on the Welsh borders, but it is still Shropshire, it is called Springhill". I wake up in the middle of the night, nudge Mame and say "why don't we buy Roger's house in Baschurch, we have always loved Shropshire, and it would be great to go back". That, of course, is me, always restless, always looking for new things to do, always seeking new horizons.

Mame is none too good; from chiding me over my many, many illnesses over the years she goes from never being ill herself to suddenly being diagnosed with breast cancer, has lumps removed, loads of radiotherapy, and gets put on a new drug, Tamoxifen, which probably saved her life, however it is my opinion that the radiotherapy, which can sometimes be a bit hit and miss, killed the cancer cells, but also took out a load of the surrounding tissue, especially in her shoulder. It also severely damaged her lungs. Unfortunately Mames condition worsened, and the sensible thing to do was to move from our house in Downderry, which had beautiful views of the wide sweep of Whitsand bay from Looe Island in the West, to Rame Head in the East. However it still had over twenty somewhat difficult steps from the front door to the road, and probably double this number from the road to the village. Mame was finding it more and more difficult because of her arthritis, and what was later to be diagnosed as osteoporosis.

Eventually we found a buyer for our house in Downderry, and moved to Roger's old house at Summerhill Cottages, a little hamlet a mile or so outside the quintessential Shropshire village of Baschurch. We had always been so exceptionally lucky with our neighbours wherever we lived, and we were not to be disappointed this move. Yet again we were immediately made to feel at home, and when Mames illnesses became much worse, these lovely neighbours used to cook the most beautiful meals in their own houses, and then march, quite a way sometimes, to our house, and in one instance, dressed up as French waiters and waitress's. This was so helpful as I had gone also down again with yet more illness, this time it was my joints as my sporting days finally caught up with me, and I needed two new hips and half a knee whilst at the same time, Mame was finding it more and more difficult to move around. Never a word of complaint from her though!

Eventually Roger called 'time' on my attempts at nursing, and suggested that we should move to a retirement flat where I could attend to Mames needs to a greater extent than that that I was achieving as a part time carer. We were though, able to have had a commendable time, when Mame was well enough, by shooting off all over the globe, not by plane as we used to do, but by jumping on board cruise ships, with Mame simply being able to put all her aches and pains out of her mind.

However a new spanner gets hurtled into that arena called daily living. The doctors kept telling me that I had a slow growing cancer in my prostate, but not to worry as old age would get me first. One day they say "oops, sorry, you are doing too well, now the cancer will probably get you before your old age". They elect to remove it but then, having been implanted with chemo drugs to lessen its growth, I do my Achilles tendon no good by first rupturing it, and then when a junior doctor failed to diagnose it, getting in to real trouble with a very severe tear, so when they do diagnose it, I find myself in a plaster cast, and then one of those 'boots' that they now use instead of a plaster cast. This means that they cannot operate on my prostate until it has healed; so the whole prostate operation was put off for over a year.

This is where luck comes in once again. At the end of that year I am offered what was was then just a trial of pinpoint radiotherapy; you are implanted with gold seeds, and the radiotherapy beam can then be operated with pinpoint accuracy, just on the cancer cells, and not damaging any of the surrounding tissue. There were around ten of us in our group, I was the oldest by far but somehow or other I am still here, but over half of those who were being treated at the same time as myself, sadly, have not made it. Well I did say earlier that one of the necessary ingredients for well-being was luck!!!

CHAPTER 27

Mame's final party

............and the greatest of these is love - Corinthians 1.13

What a send off ! ....Let's go back to around twenty years ago and recap a little, Mame is walking Bumper, that super intelligent Border Collie, each day, every day and in all weathers but, very sadly, Bumper's somewhat hectic life (a true family member!) catches up with him and we have to have him put down. Mame is now no longer walking each day. Whilst in Downderry she had decided not to continue coming to the St Mellion leisure club for swimming, as she did not like the changing rooms, did not like the appearance of varicose veins on her legs for all to see, nor for that matter, and this is particularly pertinent for all of us, just what it it is that age does to what was once a finely honed, athletic body.

The next thing was Downderry's steep hills, and those steps down to the road from the front door, and the further struggle down to the village. Maybe we ought to have somewhere where it is easier to manage, perhaps on the flat, perhaps even a flat instead of a house – maybe even a retirement home? Wow, my mistake, I should have talked her out of it, pointed out more vigorously the benefits of exercise and more importantly, the necessity of an attitude of mind that defies age as a defining limitation.

As I said at the close of the last chapter, we eventually did move to a retirement home but the oldest resident, Stanley Fielding, was coming up to his centenary. On his 100th birthday took delivery of a new motor car which he needed in order to visit his girl friend, and for delivering his lectures for fund raising for the local Rotary club of which he was a regular member, also for all the other charitable duties that he undertook. The other residents ages ranged from fifty eight upwards, but Stan seemed to have by far the youngest attitude and mind of everyone.

When we first started visiting retirement homes I managed to find something wrong with each of them. Then of course Roger rings from Moscow with his now life changing message "Dad, We've bought a farm". "OK" I say "we will buy your house" and this was when we moved to Rogers house in Baschurch in Shropshire. It was on the level, no steps, those lovely neighbours and what was to become a garden to die for; Roger and Ruth moved to their beautiful farm, "Springhill", which was only some twenty miles away, real Welsh Border country.

It does not matter where we move, Mame is fighting an uphill battle, two bouts of cancer, coupled with the most severe osteoarthritis and debilitating osteoporosis, cannot be beaten, just managed. Mame is utterly brilliant, but on the very day of the move from Baschurch to the retirement apartment at Boughton Hall in Chester, her high blood pressure, coupled with the stress of the move, leads to a burst blood vessel in her right eye, and she virtually looses all sight in that eye.

The same thing happens with the left eye, but the specialists at the Countess Hospital in Chester are superb and manage to save the sight in one eye. Had not Ruth and Roger been with her on the day of the move, and moved heaven and earth to get her specialists appointments all over Chester, then it could well have been a totally different story. We haven't been at Boughton Hall long before we have more flashing blue lights, rushing her in to A & E with suspected Encephalitis. Roger and Gaye are wonderful, all three of us take it in turns to be with her until Gaye, inner and outer strength really showing as she is taking the graveyard shift, is turned out by matron at 4.00 am.

Gaye gives up her job in Bristol in order to come up to Chester to help nurse her mother, and we all try to ensure that Mame has the best quality of life possible. When we first arrived one of the residents told me that I was a novice carer, I raised my eyebrows at this remark but she was absolutely correct, I was a novice, but after four years, the latter part being full time care, I was told that I had earned my stripes!

Those four years, which seem to have now passed so quickly, were a superb opportunity for Mame and I to really understand the true nature of love. Some couples who are not so fortunate find this period most difficult and the act of caring, which can be very difficult indeed, can drive a huge wedge between two people who had always been exceptionally close. We were extremely lucky as this period had exactly the opposite effect for us.

However it would be stupid to pretend that it was jam for tea every day. Caring of this intense nature takes it's toll but we each developed escape mechanisms. Mame by communication with old friends, and me by hurtling up and down a swimming pool. This really did seem to work miracles as we both then found exceptional enjoyment by ensuring the other persons well being.

I summed this up in in my Eulogy, but the true extent of our relationship can be found by studying the Greek words for love, and I feel that Mame and I achieved way beyond that of Agape or unselfish love. I will relate this in full in that third book, and hope, as always, as I stressed in my opening remarks, that it may be of real use to you in some small undefined way.

Mame struggled for her last four years, putting up with exceptional problems, especially breathing which she always put down, as a non smoker, to inhaling passive smoke, that is being in offices where everyone else smoked. However, in my opinion, this was brought on by the radiation treatment for her breast cancer some thirty years earlier, whereas I was extremely lucky as I had pinpoint accuracy for my cancer treatment for my prostate, but in targeting a tumour, as I postulated earlier, there is quite often damage to the surrounding tissue or bones. It certainly affected her shoulder and her lungs as well.

However she was adamant that it was from working with people who smoked, always talking of passive smoke inhalation but, personally, having seen the effects of radiation on so many cancer patients where parts of their anatomy adjacent to the cancer cells were totally destroyed or badly damaged, then I favour my thoughts on the matter. Well I would wouldn't I!!

However I do prefer Radiotherapy to Chemotherapy. When I took Mame for her first treatment in Plymouth around forty years ago, I was totally astonished at the number of patients who were seated in the waiting room. I had expected one or two but there must have been forty to fifty people present. There were always at least a dozen or so when I had my treatment, and usually it was always the same crowd. However one day I was allotted a different slot, and there was a new lady there. You did not all join at the same time, my treatment was for five days a week, for a total of six weeks, so you were constantly ticking off the number of weeks that were left until the completion of your treatment .

I turned to the new lady and asked "how long have you got left? "to which she replied "a week", "That's better than me" I said "I'm here for another three weeks". "No" she said "I was on chemo and it just became too much, so I opted to come off it, and they have only given me a week to live now, the radiotherapy is just to give me some relief from the pain". She was not despondent, she wasn't sad, simply relieved to be free of the suffering caused by the chemo.

Each case is different and the medical establishment have been brilliant in obtaining relief from cancer, but I do just hope that they understand that EVERY case is different, and that each patient has their own view. I hope that patients do not have their lives prolonged unnecessarily for what is actually, a very short period of time. Many people express the view that to see their loved ones endure unending pain, simply to prolong life for a few months is not the way for them. Having to endure extreme suffering, even if recommended by the most well meaning of health professionals, is surely not the answer.

If you wish to research this further then there are many doctors and oncologists saying exactly this. Look up a certain Dr. Greger MD FACLM, who postulates that chemo can only prolong life, in most cases, for a very short while, but imposes side effects that could be disastrous. I am a layman, I have no medical background or qualifications, I can speak only from experience, but had I known what I know now when I had my cancer treatment, then I would never have had anything to do with chemotherapy or hormone therapy, however we each have to make our own decisions on such matters; loads more details, including the ridiculous waste of money on drugs wantonly prescribed, in that next book.

Before her first bout of cancer Mame had never been that seriously ill, indeed she used to chide me as I always seemed to be the one with all the illnesses, getting everything wrong with me, however that first bout must have seriously weakened her immune system, but she never, ever, complained. Her attitude was admirable, and that carried her through when any lesser person would have succumbed. But she could see what was happening.

She did not think that she would make our 60th wedding anniversary, however somehow she did, and certainly she did not think that reaching my 85th birthday was possible, it was. Now I rarely left her unless relieved by Roger or Gaye, but she decided that she would somehow last out until her 90th. birthday. Shortly before that 90th birthday was actually upon us she said "I think I'd like a party" – impossible I thought, but Roger said "just organise it, it will give her hope".

What a party !! - she was radiant and reveled in seeing, once again, many old friends. She did not make a speech, she didn't need to, Tom, youngest grandson and I filled in, but we were no substitute, her presence said it all. A wonderful neighbour and friend made a video, hilarious. Many of her friends could not make it, too ill. George Fielding flew in from Spain, said he would not miss it, Norman and Shirley Allen and family (wonderful old neighbours from Bridgnorth), nearly made it. They should not have even set off from their home 70 miles away, far too frail and too ill. They made it as far as their Chester hotel, Norman got out of his car, fell over and ended up in Chester A&E!

Jack Pearson said he just wanted to make it to be able to say Happy Birthday to Mame, he died a few weeks later. Stan Fielding was not long after. One or two others in a similar position,

Maureen Melville made it for almost another year, but Mame's wonderful friend and brother in law, Don, had a marvelous time, he and Mame were able to have their last 'Famous Grouse' tipple together. As he was leaving he grasped my hand very, very firmly saying "best party I've ever been to". He died a four weeks later.

Mame's lovely friends were all there, Sue and Andy from Devon, Ann, Rachel and Jean from Much Wenlock, also Alan, the inspirational doctor who was for ever chiding me "when are you going to finish that book", together with his charming wife, Edna. Actually by this time they had moved a couple of miles to Homer, which is a small village just outside Much Wenlock. There were many of Mame's friends from Boughton Hall but John Young was absolutely brilliant because he filmed that super video which Mame declared as being "the icing on the cake!"

Mame got steadily worse, but she was never despondent, always cheerful and bright as a button. The real problem came in the January following the party which was held in the previous September, there was a particularly nasty bug circulating in the apartment block. Amanda, who always delivered a first class service as our 'weekly help' and myself were lucky in that our immune systems were in good working order, so we were able to get over this infection in under a week. I was quite ill, but saw just how bad that Mame was, got the doctors over, but it was only a locum that came so I rang 111, who were exceptionally efficient, and they got her into hospital immediately.

With lungs hardly working anyway, it was no wonder that she succumbed to diseases of the lungs, her breathing, difficult at the best of times, worsened, but she was superb in the way that she always, somehow, managed to cope. It was the usual performance of shifting her from ward to ward, Roger and Gaye always on hand in order that we could take it in turns to be with her. One ward was quite funny as Mame told me that, during the previous night, she had been covered in blood, could I investigate. On asking the nurse she replied "That bloody son of yours". "What are you talking about" I queried? "He brought her in all those Jaffa cakes" she said "she sat on them in the middle of the night, got covered in chocolate and it took hours to clean her up, it didn't just go over the walls, over everything else possible, we all got it in our hair as well". We all fell about laughing, except for Mame as she still continued to insist that she had been covered in blood !!

Roger, Gaye and I took it in turns to be with Mame right up until the end, this was so that one of us was always at her bedside. The nurses were efficient and understanding and the Macmillan nurses, as always, were outstanding. To be able to be with someone at this time is an exceptional privilege, and I really do not want to pre-empt volume three of this trilogy. Just let me say that Roger and Gaye's support, their love, and their general demeanor and acceptance, were something way and above just normal family ties. It was truly beautiful.

CHAPTER 28

The Meaning of Life

The best things in life are the people we love,
the places we've been and the memories we've made along the way

I once had a very funny postcard, on it was a Meditation Master with his pupil standing in front of him. The pupil asked "What is the meaning of life?", - the Master answered "Google it".

I once asked the all knowing Amazon device, Alexa, who replied "42". I couldn't fathom this out until Gaye told me that that was the reply made in the film, The Hitch-hikers Guide to the Galaxy.!! I've just asked Alexa again today, which is quite a little while since I last asked her, and she replied "be excellent to each other". I like that.

It is whatever is pertinent to you, ask six people and you will get six different answers quite a few of which will be "I haven't got a clue".

How about it just being a whole series of little hills to climb,

How about it just being little goals to achieve,

How about it just being…………

Is this KISS??

Think so

Just be

CHAPTER 29

Conclusion

Out beyond ideas of wrong doing and right doing,
there is a field, I will meet you there. - Rumi.

In her introduction Helen talked of 'occupational flow' and where I can, I have expanded this a little using my knowledge of flow such as that seen in Arthur Ashe when winning his Wimbledon singles final in June of 1975. How about a situation where you could experience this wonderful way of being all of the time? If you asked someone if they lived their life in this way and they answered 'yes', then it would be immediately lost. Why? - please let me explain by way of an analogy:

You are a talented artist and one day you chip away at a block of ice and come up with a masterpiece. You are very proud of your work and put it on display for all to see. Everyone marvels at your work, your masterpiece, and heaps much praise upon you, but then something strange happens, it starts to disappear, it melts. Finally you are left with a pool of water. In other words you cannot achieve that deep contentment that you may have noticed exuding from those that have it by seeking it or trying to learn about it, if it is going to happen then it will, if not it wont. My belief is that it can only be achieved by not seeking it, and simply living a life of service to others. Then allow it to come entirely of it's own accord, if it so wishes.

I hope that makes sense, if not then I'm a lousy writer and an even worse communicator! So let me expand a little; if you asked someone whom you think leads such a life, let us say H.H the Dali Lama, the reply would be one of his famous chuckles and a possible reply of "I am just a simple Buddhist monk". You have to 'become' that state and it cannot be obtained without a very, very solid base of *Sila* or virtue which I mentioned earlier, however, once obtained, everything else becomes redundant. *Including whether you have achieved it or not.* However if you do get anywhere remotely near to that state, or even if you can just experience 'flow', just once, in the way described by Helen in her introduction then you will have achieved much.

It is not possible to say "do this" and "do that". In one of my opening paragraphs I said that I had no magic wand, no way of giving some trite answers than can be copied, the only thing that I could do would be to lay out what I did to help myself, just pick from it what you think will help you, or simply make your own list, so please let me conclude by simply running over those 'tools' that I use, and which may be of help to you.

I get out in the fresh air, among trees, among nature.

I express my gratitude, firstly for just being alive!

I try to live purely 'in the moment'.

I have a wonderful numbers of play lists and listen to music, which if not playing on a device, then I play in my head.

I also have marvelous times of pure silence.

I offer kindness and help wherever I can – and sometimes get into terrible trouble when offered in the wrong place.

I simply accept those situations, no matter how grim that they might appear to someone else, that I cannot change. And accept them with pleasure.

I trust that I have no attachment to any idea, concept, possession or indeed to life itself.

I endeavour to love with all my heart, BUT it is with unconditional or agape love.

I use too many 'I's.

Dave Allen used to end all his shows with 'may your God go with you' - nice line.

Have fun !!

Epilogue

Let us visualize, let's create a picture; you have wonderful, total peace, tranquility, happiness, and let us also suppose that you are surrounded by nature; that you have many kinds of birds all around you, especially the robins and blackbirds but you also have some wild rabbits with all their children, you even see some tiny newts. All come to share in an idyllic moment that will last for ever, total happiness; you may be sitting in a garden at the end of the day with all your gardening completed. Perhaps, somehow or other, you have managed to find a glass of wine at your elbow. You are surrounded by trees, flowers, bushes, by nature in all her kindness, you have total, utter peace. To you it seems that this will last for ever.

Hang on……….

No it doesn't, remember those people for whom everything is perfect, well adjusted, in control and then the unexpected happens? It happens to all of us so the real key is survival. Above all learn to survive, hopefully some of that survival kit may have just been read, but if you do get those moments such as total and complete peace, then do remember them, and savour the moments, for you can reach them, and with much greater ease, if you continually practice kindness, think always of others, put yourself last, be true to yourself, and above all, do endeavour to love – with unconditional agape love you will always have every help possible – and true happiness. Have fun and live forever.

As long as space endures
As long as sentient beings remain
May I too abide
And dispel the miseries of the world

Prayer by Shantideva as quoted by HH the Dalai Lama
when he received his Nobel Peace Prize in Oslo on December 10th 1989.

BV - #0022 - 120723 - C0 - 216/140/9 - PB - 9781915972057 - Gloss Lamination